# Reaching for
# the Stars

# Reaching for the Stars

*The Inspiring Story of a Migrant Farmworker*
*Turned Astronaut*

José M. Hernández

Foreword by Emilio Estefan

**CENTER**
**STREET**
New York   Boston   Nashville

Unless otherwise noted, all photos are from the author's personal collection.

Center Street
Hachette Book Group
237 Park Avenue
New York, NY 10017

www.CenterStreet.com

Printed in the United States of America

RRD-C

First edition: September 2012
10  9  8  7  6  5  4  3

Center Street is a division of Hachette Book Group, Inc.
The Center Street name and logo are trademarks of Hachette Book Group, Inc.

The Hachette Speakers Bureau provides a wide range of authors for speaking events. To find out more, go to www.HachetteSpeakersBureau.com or call (866) 376-6591.

The publisher is not responsible for websites (or their content) that are not owned by the publisher.

LCCN: 2012939937

ISBN: 978-1-4555-2280-4

*This book is dedicated to all the children*
*who look up in the sky at the stars*
*and envision a better tomorrow—not just for themselves,*
*but for the world.*

# Acknowledgments

How does a person say thank you when he has a lifetime's worth of people to thank? I have been blessed to have had so many astounding people who have crossed my path and helped me achieve my dream to reach the stars.

Education has played a vital role in making me who I am today. For that, I have to thank those educators who believed in me and who tirelessly worked to make me believe in myself. I am grateful to my second grade teacher, Ms. Marlesse Young, who gave me my first astronomy book and who was the first person to stand up for my future. To Mrs. Sylvia Bello, my Spanish and biology teacher, and to Mr. David Ellis, my math instructor and a superb racquetball player, I offer my heartfelt thanks. I wish I could have expressed my gratitude to the late Mr. Salvador Zendejas, my high school history teacher, who taught me to embrace my culture. I truly appreciate Mr. Vance Paulsen, my high school counselor, for giving me my first real paying job at the Tillie Lewis Cannery. I also wish the late Dr. Andrés Rodríguez, my college physics professor, could know how much it meant for him to teach me to keep my chin up.

Professionally, I have been so lucky to have been surrounded by such amazing mentors, as well as such energetic and successful coworkers. Mr. Frank Inami, the recruiter at Lawrence Livermore National Laboratory, took a chance on me and that has made all the difference in my life. As the laboratory's engineering director of diversity, Ms. Shirley McDavid coached me throughout my career at the laboratory; in the process, I happily came to consider her as my second mother. I am incredibly grateful to Mr. Clint Logan, my mentor and good friend, for having the foresight to see the medical applications of our X-ray laser research and for allowing me to play a part in developing lifesaving technology. I appreciate the time Clint spent using a red pen to review the technical details of our work in the manuscript. Thank you also to my first boss at NASA, Ms. Irene Kaye, who challenged me to do my best.

I would like to express my deep appreciation to members of my family who have nurtured, supported, loved, and encouraged me my whole life. I learned so much from each of my siblings—all of whom are older than me. Their advice throughout my schooling was invaluable. My oldest brother, Salvador Jr., set the educational achievement bar for the rest of us siblings to reach. I try to follow in the example of my sister, Leticia, who has done a wonderful job raising a wonderful family. And, of course, I am happy to vicariously live through my free-spirited eternal bachelor of a brother, Gil. I would like to thank Salvador and Julia, the two people who—in spite of having just a third grade education—were expert motivators. My parents not only managed to give their four children a college education, but they also gave their youngest the license to dream. Words could never truly express my gratitude for their belief in me, and I do not know what I would have done without their recipe to achieve what would have otherwise seemed impossible. My beautiful wife, Adela, has crisscrossed the country with me in search of my dream, and I know how lucky I am to have her in my life. She is, without a doubt, the foundation that keeps our family solidly grounded. I thank my son Julio, who is wise beyond his years; Karina, for being so nurturing; Vanessa, for being so much like me; Yesenia, for academically challenging the rest of her siblings; and Antonio, for his promise to take care of Adela and me when we get old. You kids really make us look like excellent parents!

Finally, I would like to thank the folks related to the creation of this book. Thanks to Oprah Winfrey, who—after interviewing me on her show—suggested I write a book to tell my story, and to world-renowned Spanish-language reporter and commentator Mr. Jorge Ramos. I am thankful for my good friend Emilio Estefan, who so kindly agreed to write the Foreword. An enormous amount of gratitude is owed to my fellow Pacific alum and aspiring writer/director Jorge Ramirez-Martinez for diligently helping me with the composition of my stories. To the talented Emilia Pablo-Montaño, who helped put the finishing touches on this book, I offer my sincere thanks. Last but not least, thanks to Jennifer Wadsworth for devoting herself to meticulously editing the manuscript and for providing intelligent, insightful suggestions that have helped me share my story with all of you in the best way I can.

# Contents

# Author's Note

This is my story and I've recorded it here to the best of my recollection. I thank all the people who touched my life and helped me achieve my dreams and I have tried to accurately portray our conversations and time together.

# Foreword

## by Emilio Estefan

It is my honor to be able to introduce José Hernández's amazing story of hard work, perseverance, and determination. When he reached the stars, he had no idea how many of us he was taking along with him on his journey.

The foundation of his story begins with his parents, so I would like to start by congratulating them for all the sacrifices they made for José and for the rest of their family. I strongly believe it is their example that both inspired José's insatiable drive to achieve his dreams and contributed to his love for his family, his wife, and his children.

José is living proof that there are no barriers that should hold anyone back from setting and achieving goals in life. José began learning English at twelve years old; yet, he attained a degree in engineering that led to research that consequently helped so many by astonishingly contributing to the early detection of cancer. Furthermore, he did not let numerous rejections from the National Aeronautics and Space Administration (NASA) get in the way of reaching for the stars, and he became the first astronaut to tweet *en español* from space.

José, we are all proud of you! You are a great example, not only for Latinos, but also for other ethnic minority groups all over the world who struggle every day to make their dreams a reality.

Who would have thought that a kid who helped his parents

harvest this land with his bare hands would be sowing his own legacy? Who could have ever guessed that same child would one day shake the hand of the President of the United States after being honored for his astounding achievements and contributions to this great country? José, you are a true representation of the American Dream.

I feel proud not only to call you, José Hernández, an astronaut, but also to call you my Mexican American friend.

Congratulations on both an incredible journey and an incredible book!

# Reaching for
# the Stars

# CHAPTER 1
# About My Father

*Where we love is home—home that our feet may leave,*
*but not our hearts.*

OLIVER WENDELL HOLMES (1809–1894)
AMERICAN POET AND HUMORIST

The story of my father, Salvador, is written in the *surcos*, known as furrows, of the fields in central Mexico in the state of Michoacán. He was only seven years old when he began plowing the same fertile lands as his ancestors. He and my grandfather José—for whom I was named—were like many of their fellow countrymen; the two were peasant workers who made a living sowing and harvesting small plots of land. They lived in small homes made of *adobe*, the same packed earth on which their very livelihood depended. They lived in harmony with farm animals under the blue, majestic Michoacán sky.

My *abuelo*, or grandfather, lived in Ticuítaco, a small village, or *rancheria*, located near the municipality of La Piedad. The calmness of the days and nights can be seen as either a blessing or a punishment by the village's citizens, who, depending on their mood, thanked God for the tranquility they breathed or cursed the stillness in which they lived. It is precisely in this town and environment where my father was born and raised. It is also the place where, as a child, he began to work. He knew that his family depended on his work in the fields, or *los campos*, to survive. This is where everything began; like a seed that germinates, my life story has its roots in the Mexican soil of the state of Michoacán.

In 1944, things were not easy for the male peasant workers of Ticuítaco. The harsh reality was that their wives and children also faced the burden of making money through menial labor to provide for their families. Although my father was young at the time, he was aware of the circumstances that surrounded him and he knew he had a responsibility. He began to work the fields to help support his parents and eleven siblings.

A typical workday for my father, with few exceptions, began at four in the morning. He would start his day by feeding the animals in my *abuelo*'s stable, known as the *corrales*. This consisted of washing the pigpens, refilling the water troughs, and feeding the pigs. Next, he would release the chickens and turkeys before spreading their daily seed for them to feed upon. Finally, my father would corral the cows, which would join a herd that would graze the open pastures just outside of Ticuítaco. The boys in the neighborhood would take turns taking care of the large multifamily herd. Upon finishing these initial tasks, assuming it was not his turn to tend to the community herd, my father would then join my grandfather in the kitchen.

The kitchen was where Cleotilde, my grandmother, or *abuela*, would prepare the breakfast and lunch for my *abuelo* and the older boys. The breakfast was very simple; a hot chocolate with two or three corn tortillas right off the hot skillet, known as a *comal*, was served with beans and a healthy dose of chile that was prepared directly on a *molcajete*. A *molcajete* is a bowl with three legs sculpted out of lava rock. These *molcajetes*, as I would later learn, were made by nearby indigenous

Tarascans. After finishing breakfast, my *abuela* would then pack a lunch for my grandfather, my father, and my *tíos*, or uncles. The lunch consisted of a healthier portion of the breakfast items and was usually garnished with a piece of meat. My *abuela* would fit everything in a small, colorful, nylon-weaved bag with plastic handles known as an *hargana*.

Then, my father and his older siblings would follow my *abuelo* into the fields where plowing and harvesting awaited them, day after day. Despite working in the *campo* from sunup to sundown, without having much time to dedicate to his schooling, my father's desire to learn how to read and write was strong. This led him to enroll in evening sessions of the school near the house where he lived. He loved school so much that he never missed a day of class. However, as he grew, so did his responsibilities at home; eventually, that led to his inability to attend school beyond the third grade. This is a common story for the majority of the children of Ticuítaco, including my mother.

My father had many dreams and goals at a very young age, and he did everything in his power to make them a reality. My siblings and I grew up listening to my father talk about the challenges and obstacles he faced as a child. His anecdotes taught us lessons about overcoming adversity. Those stories remain dear to me.

At the tender age of ten, my father was the fare collector of the only *camión*, or bus, that took passengers to and from Ticuítaco to La Piedad. The *camión* was graciously christened "*El Muchacho Alegre*," or "The Happy Youngster." It made only one trip into town a day, except on holidays when it would make two. The driver of the *camión*, Don Severiano

Arroyo, noticed my father's eagerness to better his life and his future. So it came as no surprise to Don Severiano when my father asked him, "Can you teach me how to drive your *camión*?"

"Don't be silly, boy, you can't even reach the pedals!" said Don Severiano.

"Come on, please. I've seen you drive and it doesn't look difficult...please," insisted Salvador.

My father was extremely persistent; he would ask Mr. Severiano to teach him how to drive every day. Salvador insisted and insisted until Mr. Severiano finally agreed. Even though my father could barely reach the gas and brake pedals with the tips of his toes, he quickly learned how to maneuver *El Muchacho Alegre* through the narrow streets, or *callejones*, of Ticuítaco and into the bigger and wider streets of La Piedad.

Time passed with no opportunity for anyone to forge a better future in the hope of overcoming the poverty and hopelessness that consumed La Piedad and its surroundings; nevertheless, my father had a plan. When he reached fifteen years old, he made a decision that would change the rest of his life and that of his future family—for the better!

"*Papá*, I've decided to move to the United States" is what my father said to my *abuelo* as he fed the pigs in the *corrales*.

"May I ask why all of a sudden?" sullenly asked my *abuelo*. "You have everything here...am I wrong?"

"You're right, but the fields do not yield what they used to before, and there is hardly any work and money," responded Salvador.

"So, do you plan on returning?" inquired my grandfather.

"Well, I'm going to test my luck. I've already spoken with

my friend Eliseo and he has agreed to come with me. We're going to California."

My *abuelo* did not know how to take the news of his son leaving for the United States. *Abuelo* already had three sons who had ventured off in search of a better life—he didn't want to be apart from one more. Therefore, letting go of Salvador would not be easy, but *Abuelo* felt that he had no choice in the matter after realizing his son's determination and stubbornness.

"I suppose there isn't anything I can do or say to persuade you to stay, since you've already made up your mind. *Ay muchacho*, you have my blessing to go. If things don't go as planned, you're always welcome to come back home. I'm going to give you some money to hold you over until you find work." My *abuelo* did not know what else to say.

With three hundred *pesos* in his pocket, my father and Eliseo set out on their journey. Eliseo was the same age as my father. His strong Tarascan complexion and characteristics were inherited directly from the indigenous ancestors of their land. Eliseo's parents and my grandparents had been friends for decades, so it was no surprise that Eliseo and Salvador became such good friends. Their families' connections to one another just made their bond all the more special.

In 1952, the controversial hot topic being discussed in the streets of La Piedad concerned the "economic progress and growth" of Mexico. According to the elderly people of that time, opportunities for the rural poor were nonexistent. In the state of Michoacán and outside of small *ciudades*, or cities, like La Piedad, there were only a few paved roads for *camiónes* to steer through; it was a luxury to drive on paved roads. The pathways consisted of nothing more than dirt and rocks, although in some spots there was evidence of an attempt to improve the ground with a layer of reddish, sandlike texture. Unfortunately, only the donkeys and cows seemed to have benefited from the limited street enhancements. The livestock would roam along the obstacle-free roadways, leaving behind footprints and manure as they paraded with a red cloud of dirt trailing behind them. Few people traveled to or visited nearby villages without having the money to safely or comfortably get from one place to another.

Eliseo and Salvador hoped to escape that poverty by migrating to the north. Touring through the vast, dry land, the two men were accompanied by thirst, hunger, and occasional uncertainty. After a month—which, according to them, seemed more like a century—they finally reached the border, or *la frontera*. My father had only a few *pesos* left over from the three hundred he originally had when he started his journey. According to my father, it was barely enough for a plate of beans.

Eliseo addressed my father as Chava, a common nickname for the name Salvador. "Chava, don't you think we should go back? Look at us, Chava; we're getting skinnier by the passing of each day!"

"We only have a little ways to go. We'll be there in a few days," answered my father.

"But I'm afraid we may not make it, Chava. I feel weak and we are running out of money!" said Eliseo, more worried than ever before.

"Tell you what, Eliseo: we'll rest here a bit and then we'll continue."

My father remembers sitting with Eliseo on a sidewalk in

front of a store in Mexicali, a city located near the U.S.-Mexico border. He remembers being extremely exhausted, having to camouflage his tiredness with courage and optimism to continue moving forward. Chava refused to let Eliseo see him weak or defeated. Chava was determined to cross over to the United States. As for Eliseo, he had no choice but to continue the journey, despite having his feet covered with blisters; these sores were the result of walking the hot terrain in a worn-out pair of leather sandals known as *huaraches*. At this point, the men were beginning to experience, on a daily basis, dryness in their mouths from the lack of water that reached their lips. This was coupled with emptiness in their stomachs from going without food.

"I couldn't help but overhear you two *muchachos* conversing. Are you two headed for *El Norte*?" asked a man who was standing at the entrance of the store. *El Norte* was the common term used for the United States.

Eliseo was quick to respond, *"Sí, señor."*

"And may I ask where to?" inquired the man.

The truth is that neither Eliseo nor Chava knew how to respond because neither knew where their trip would end. All they knew was that my father had a *primo*, or cousin, living on a ranch near Fresno, California. They had hoped to stay with that cousin, but they were not certain that would be a possibility.

"Well, honestly, we really don't know where we're headed to. I guess we'll figure it out once we get there."

*"Ay muchachos*, I imagined so. My name is Juan Mora. I'm from Michoacán and I work in the fields of Fresno. I take it you two are a long ways from home and with no money."

"Nice to meet you," said my father as he extended his right hand to Juan Mora. "We're also from Michoacán," my father added.

"Come, I'm going to take you two to get some food, and we can figure out a plan to find you guys some *trabajo*." *Trabajo* is the Spanish word for "work."

The life of a migrant worker was not an easy one, especially as an undocumented immigrant. Both my father and Eliseo were well aware of this, but they did not care because they knew that this alternative was much more promising than their way of life back in Michoacán. *El Norte* was the only hope for prosperity in exchange for their hard work, and they were not going to allow anything to deter them from succeeding.

Juan Mora helped Salvador and Eliseo complete their journey to a small ranch located in the outskirts of Fresno, California. My father and Eliseo quickly found work as seasonal agricultural workers; more important, they were paid in U.S. dollars. The majority of the fieldworkers in the surrounding fields were fellow *Mexicanos* who picked fruits and vegetables from sunrise to sunset. The two of them did not earn much, but in comparison to what they made in Mexico, it was far more than they ever imagined.

My father spent the next two and a half years working the fertile fields of California's San Joaquin Valley, harvesting everything from strawberries to cucumbers in the summer, and pruning trees and grapevines in the winter. Later in life, I would remember the result of his arduous work each time I touched his tough, rough, and leathery hands. After thirty months of doing rigorous work for long hours in the sun, my father had managed to save enough money to return home to a special someone. This special person was Julia, a fourteen-year-old girl who was born and raised in the *rancho* of Ticuítaco, just like my father. Julia naturally possessed a simple beauty that was accentuated by her brown eyes, light complexion, and eternal smile. Years later, this beautiful girl would become my mother.

Since my mother was practically a child, her family prohibited her from having a boyfriend. This tended to be the norm in small towns like La Piedad. Therefore, my mother was always under the supervision of one of my *tíos*, which made it impossible for her to catch a glimpse of, or be alone with, my father. However, when it comes to love, anything is possible. My parents are living proof of it.

My parents met at the kiosk, which was directly across from the main church, by the city hall, in the center of town known as the *plaza*. Traditionally, all the young, single ladies would put on their most beautiful dresses to walk together, in a group, clockwise around the *plaza* on Sundays. Going counterclockwise were the young suitors of La Piedad and the surrounding *rancherías*. The men would walk in the opposite direction, eyeing the young ladies they liked; this allowed them to exchange looks with one another. When a young suitor discovered "the one," he would present a rose to her. If the lady accepted the rose, this would signal the start of her courtship with the young man. This was how my parents met and began their life together.

Unfortunately for my father, my maternal grandparents— Trinidad and Rosario Moreno, or *Trini y Chayito*, as they were affectionately called—were extremely old-fashioned and strict. My mother was under constant supervision and rarely had the opportunity to head to the town square with her girlfriends. Soon, my mother's parents became aware of my father's existence. All they knew was that Salvador was the son of a nice and decent *campesino*, or peasant family, from Ticuítaco.

Both Julia and Salvador decided to start a relationship despite the disapproval of my *abuelo*. On many occasions, *abuelo* chased away my father at gunpoint. *Abuelo* was not about to lose his precious daughter to Salvador. Therefore, my parents had to find time to be together free of the watchful eyes of Julia's parents. When they did, they showed affection by gazing at each other and intermittently holding hands; in addition, they secretly wrote letters, or *cartitas*, in which they expressed their love for each other.

After spending a significant amount of time in *El Norte*, my father—who left as a boy—returned home as a young man. He was building the foundation of a future in which he could provide for Julia. With this conviction, he decided to ask for my mother's hand in marriage, and he did so at his own risk. He was fully aware of my grandfather's willingness to scare him off the property at gunpoint, yet Salvador was willing to take that chance because he loved my mother and he did not want to spend his days without her. Hoping to be taken seriously, and out of respect, he had the town priest accompany him to meet with Julia's father.

"Mr. Trinidad, this young man here loves your daughter, and he has nothing but the best intentions for her," the priest quickly blurted when my grandfather opened the door.

"I don't care. I've said it once, and I'll say it again. Julia is way too young to get married. Don't you understand?" my grandfather responded while pointing angrily at my father.

"Look, Trinidad, they are both in love, and he respects her. I know she's young. Don't cause them to be apart and miserable. Think about it: he is a hard worker and, just like you, he makes an honest living in the fields. Backbreaking, honest work is what real honorable men are made of, you know that," said the priest.

The angry look on my grandfather's face soon gave way to what appeared to be resignation to the fact that his daughter would soon marry. Although not completely convinced, he allowed the priest and my father to enter his house for twenty minutes. My father did not say much, for his future father-in-law's presence made him forget what he had been practicing to say for months.

"Why did you come with him, Father?" asked Trinidad with a visible frown.

"Because I've known him and his family for many years, and we all know you threatened him with a gun so he would stay away from your daughter. I'd rather be safe than sorry, Trinidad," answered the priest.

"I want the best for my daughter, and I don't think having a boyfriend or getting married is right for her at this moment," said Trinidad to both of them.

"I understand, but nowadays to find a son-in-law like Salvador is not as easy as it used to be," responded the priest to my grandfather, who turned suspiciously to my father and asked: "What do you have to say for yourself?"

Unsure of what to do or say, my father got up from his seat, walked over to my grandfather, looked him in the eyes, and said, "I love your daughter more than anything in this world, and I will do anything you ask until you see that I am worthy of marrying her."

My grandfather saw the sincerity and honesty in my father's eyes, which made it more difficult for him to disapprove of my father. As a result of this visit, Trinidad gave my father and mother permission to court each other as long as they were under the family's supervision. Their first conversation as a couple took place in my mother's house; it was short and straight to the point.

"Julia," said my father as he took her hand. "I'm leaving again for the U.S. so that I can make enough money for us to get married and live together forever."

"How much time are we talking about, Salvador? When do you plan on coming back?" inquired my mother.

"I don't know. Not long, I hope. We're engaged, that's all that matters now."

"True, but you might meet someone over there. What then?"

"Well..."

"No, I'll give you eight months to come back, Salvador. If you don't come, our engagement will be over," replied Julia firmly as she shut the door on him.

My father concurred. This time around, he planned on working only eight months in the United States. Not a day went by in which he did not count down the remaining days until he could return home to marry Julia.

These fond memories of my father and mother hold vestiges of an era that was difficult yet had a peculiar charm. When I was a child, my father kept us entertained with his stories. He would tell us that in his day, no one could really afford a television in Mexico. That was why many people would stand outside of storefront windows to watch the black-and-white images being transmitted on the television monitors. He vividly remembers having watched his first Rose Parade in 1954. He recalls the streets of Pasadena, California, lined with the cars that were decorated with colorful, fresh flowers that represented animals, caricatures, scenes from films, and prominent figures. He noticed, via the television, that the spectacle captivated the people watching it in person. My father lacked the financial means to actually travel and see it in person, but told me that he anxiously awaited every January 1 to watch the parade on television. He said the parade was the most beautiful event he had ever seen in his entire life.

Julia waited in Ticuítaco for her future husband. She was hopeful that he would keep his promise and return for her. Their young love remained strong as ever, and—after being apart for months—the day finally came when they exchanged vows in front of their families in a delightful and humble ceremony.

There are few memories of that simple wedding; many of the details have been blurred by the passage of time and the creation of new memories. I, for example, can only remember my maternal grandfather, Trinidad, by the photographs that I have of him. I cannot recall a hug or a kiss from him because he died when I was only two years old. His tuberculosis proved to be the only thing that could permanently yank his roots from Ticuítaco. He caught the disease on one of his own trips in search of work in northern Mexico, near Ensenada, where he slept in close proximity to his coworkers in a little house made of straw. "The life of a *campesino* is a hard one" is what my grandfather would tell his children, including my mother. This is true, especially when one loves his homeland but must leave it in search of a better life.

My brother Salvador remembers my *abuelos*, or grandparents, much better than I do because he was my parents' firstborn. Not only was he the joy of the whole family, but he was also able to share special moments with my *abuelos*. Two years after his birth, my sister, Leticia, was born. It was not until my mother conceived my third sibling, Gilberto, that my parents decided to apply for their papers, or *papeles*, to legally work and live in the United States.

I was born on August 7, 1962, in French Camp, California. At that time, my family lived in Stockton, California. That is where the story of my life begins. I grew up surrounded by the love of my family and the many hardships that come along with being part of a migrant family. My memory begins at the age of five, precisely at the time I started school.

# CHAPTER 2
# The Seed Germinates

*If the seed is planted with faith and watered with persever-*
*ance, it will only be a matter of time before it flourishes.*
THOMAS CARLYLE (1795–1881)
SCOTTISH HISTORIAN AND ESSAYIST

Many years have passed since I first started school, but those first few days have remained fresh in my memory. I still remember not understanding the importance of having to go to school. It seemed so strange and out of the ordinary to have to get up so early every morning to take a yellow bus, known to us as *el camión amarillo*, to school; it was especially strange to be surrounded by so many other children who spoke English, which at the time I did not understand.

I remember boarding this bus to school when we were living out in the countryside near the city of Modesto. The school, located in the small town of Salida, seemed very large and was filled with students who seemed a lot bigger and older than me. The classrooms were decorated and filled with rows of shiny new desks; the desks had built-in compartments that allowed us to store our pencils, crayons, and papers. I could not believe I was assigned my own beautiful desk. Phrases of gratitude were silently running through my head, but all I could do was stare at the blackboard because I did not speak the language. I tried to figure out the meaning of what was written and drawn in colored chalk. I never dared to raise my hand to ask a question, let alone answer one. I also never fully participated in any of the classroom kindergarten activities like singing, storytelling, or playing board games. It came as no surprise that my kindergarten teacher, whom I called *la maestra*, spoke only English. She was not sure I understood everything that was being taught, much less being said. I remained silent with the hope of being invisible to everyone.

Although I did not speak English, or *inglés*, that did not keep me from having fun during my lunch hour and recess, or *recreo*, as I called it. I was just a kid who had fun whenever I had the opportunity. For example, I was very happy when it came time to play a sport! I was content when we got to play *fútbol*, or soccer, because it was an occasion where I did not have to master English—just the ball. I was a good soccer player, or at least that was what my classmates made me think. Whenever the captain of each team started to select the players for his side, both captains always wanted to be the first to select me. Those moments would be the first times I ever felt a sense of belonging at school, giving me the motivation to get up every morning and catch the *camión amarillo*.

With the exception of recess and lunch, every day consisted of the same thing as the prior day: vocabulary words that were foreign to me, coupled with stares at my brown complexion from classmates with blue eyes and light skin. I knew perfectly well that my outward appearance differed from that of the rest of the kids at my school; however, when I complained to my father about it, he always told me that everyone in the world was equally the same, period.

I remember a specific incident that happened to me one day as I was walking to the bus after school. James, a fellow classmate, closely observed what I had brought for lunch before calling me a *come tacos*, or taco eater. After seeing my homemade tacos, James's facial expression was full of disgust. To this day, I cannot get the image of his face out of my mind. I remember every detail: his mouth bent into a frown, his nose wrinkled like an accordion, and his eyebrows suddenly closer together. At that time, I did not pay too much attention to him, and I continued eating my lunch while thinking: "What does *come tacos* mean? Is it a bad thing to eat tacos? The tacos that my mom prepared for me look a lot more delicious than the bologna sandwich he is eating."

Trying to forget James's reaction to my packed lunch, I went on with my life, giving little importance to his expressions or comments. I was always happy to come home every day after school. When my siblings and I stepped inside our home, I would scream, "*Mamá*, we're home!"

"Okay. Wash your hands and do your homework. Dinner is almost ready and your father is about to come home," *Mamá* would reply.

"Okay, *Mamá*," I would scream at the top of my lungs.

Chava, Lety, and Gil—my siblings—were always right behind me like a military lineup; together we marched through the door every single day after school. Chavita, as we called him out of affection, was the oldest. He was responsible for protecting his three younger siblings. Lety, my parents' only daughter, was vivacious and full of life. At eight years old, she was the one who helped my mother take care of *los hombres de la casa*, or the men of the house. Gil, who was two years younger than Lety, was the liveliest of the four of us, a real whirlwind. As for me, I was just like any five-year-old, always exploring and full of unanswered questions. What I loved to do most as a kid was to play *fútbol* and spend the afternoons watching television with my parents, or *papás,* as I called them. I, of course, had another passion that I did not mention to anyone for quite some time...

In spite of my inquisitive nature, I remained focused on the daily activities at school and at home. Every day, as *Mamá* prepared dinner and the fresh flour handmade tortillas, my siblings and I sat around the kitchen table with our books open as we simultaneously inhaled the fragrant smell of dinner. We would hurry to finish our homework—or *la tarea,* as *Mamá* called it—because once we finished it, we could go play or watch television. That was our motivation to do our work.

> Homework:
> Problem number 1: 2 + 3 = 5
> Problem number 2: If there are seven apples, and a boy decides to eat one, how many are left? There are only six apples left.

*I understand this completely!* I thought to myself, with a smile on my face, every time I did my math homework. Sadly, this was not the case when it came to my English homework.

> I am...
> You are...

"Why the long face?" asked my father as he arrived from work and walked into the kitchen with a sense of curiosity.

"I don't understand anything at school because I don't speak English. It's really hard for me."

"I've already told you: if you live in the United States, you have to learn English. You can't just give up," my dad would say with encouragement.

"But we're going to go back to Michoacán in a month. Can I stay home tomorrow, *Papá*? It's Friday."

"No, no, no," he said as he ran his hand through my hair affectionately. "Go on, finish your homework. I know it's difficult, but I also know you're capable of doing it—and much more. You just have to put your mind to it."

Since my family and I were migrant workers, known as *campesinos*, we traveled to the U.S. from Mexico following the harvest throughout California. We migrated from one house to another in different cities within the San Joaquin Valley, which comprises most of central California. We spent the majority of our time near Stockton, California, where we worked in *los campos* during the cucumber, cherry, strawberry, peach, tomato, and grape seasons. In fact, we worked on any and every fruit and vegetable crop that needed harvesting.

Our family would drive from La Piedad, Michoacán, to California in February of each year, so we could spend the spring and summer in the U.S. Then, halfway through the fall, usually around mid-November, we would pack up all of our belongings and make the long two-and-a-half-day trip back to Mexico. We would spend the rest of the fall season and the entire winter with our extended family in La Piedad. The next year when February came around, the cycle would repeat, and we would find ourselves making the same stops and usually renting the same houses in California. Once again, we moved from one city to another. Our routes were so well established that we typically returned to work with the same contractor, or *contratista*, working for the same farmers and in the same fields, year after year.

La Piedad, Michoacán, and its surroundings have always been known for the flow of migrant workers leaving to come to the United States. Most workers labor in the fields of California before returning to their hometowns to buy plots of land to build houses on for their families. The construction of such a house usually takes years to complete as family members pool their yearly earnings together for its building. I still remember the plot of land my father bought and the many years it took for us to finish our house. During our stay in Mexico each year, my father would hire one or two skilled bricklayers known as *maestros*. We kids, known in the construction industry as *peones*, would mix the cement with shovels, and bring both cement and bricks to the *maestro* for him to work his magic in constructing the walls of our future home.

When our family was back in the United States, regardless of the city we were living in, I continued attending school and doing my homework with the encouragement of my father and mother. Of course they would check to ensure I did indeed finish my homework. It only took once for me to get caught fibbing to them that I had completed my work to realize that my parents were serious about us kids finishing our assignments. I still remember the whipping my father gave me for telling that lie! Chavita, Lety, and Gil somehow always managed to finish their homework before me and move on to their chores, or *quehaceres*. Every day they would be first to gather around the screen of our small black-and-white television set. I remember that television vividly. It was the bulky wooden console type, which was held up like a piece of furniture by four short and skinny legs; the screen was in the middle, surrounded by speakers on each side, and there were big knobs for changing the channel and a "bunny ear" antenna to help improve reception. I would hear Lety yell from the living room, "Pepito! Hurry up! *Star Trek* is about to start." *Pepito* is a term of endearment for young boys who are named José. Once an adolescent, the term would typically change to *Pepe*.

"I'm coming, I'm coming," I would yell back.

Then, a few seconds later, I would hear, "Pepito! It's starting."

So, I would run straight into the living room, leaving my homework completed but still laid out on the kitchen table.

*Star Trek* was my favorite show growing up. My brother Chava had a toy model of the USS *Enterprise* spaceship from the show, which was my favorite toy to borrow and play with for hours and hours. While playing with it, I would disregard the ticking of the clock and would go into deep concentration on the clouds, stars, and planets, as well as the vastness of the open blue sky. Those thoughts captivated my mind to the point where I could not stop thinking about them, even when I stopped playing with my brother's toy model.

"Look, they're in the spaceship on their way to the planet Ghorusda, and they say the mission is going to be hard because the inhabitants of the planet are dangerous. I wonder what's going to happen," I said, wanting to know right away.

"Pepito, we can't see anything on the TV. Can you adjust the antenna so we can watch the show?" my sister asked.

Whenever our *televisión* had poor, snowy reception—which happened frequently—I was put in charge of fixing the problem. Somehow I was always tasked with adjusting the rabbit ear antenna. With my help, the image quality would greatly improve and my siblings would ask me to me stay there while they enjoyed a new episode of *Star Trek*; I always found this to be unfortunate. I was only able to catch glimpses of the intergalactic spaceships, distant planets, and stars while still holding the antenna. I now tease my siblings and tell them that it was through osmosis that I became an astronaut because I always had to hold the antenna when any space-themed program was on TV. I add that they too could have become astronauts if only they had helped me adjust the antenna.

In Stockton—where we spent the majority of the year while in California—we lived in a small, rented three-bedroom house located on the east side of town. It was an old house made of wood with a tile roof. It had a small bathroom, a round dining table, and a living room with old furniture. Although the kitchen was small, it was always stocked with the necessities for making a delicious Mexican meal: tortillas, tomatoes, peppers, and onions. The *cuarto*, or bedroom, I shared with Chava and Gil had only two beds, a desk, and a dresser. Our furniture was rather austere and most of the pieces were secondhand. The most luxurious item my family owned was the black-and-white television set, and even that was old by normal standards. The street we lived on reflected the humbleness of its residents, my family included. With few exceptions, my neighbors made a living working either in *los campos* or *las canerias*, in the fields or the canneries. The canneries process vegetables and fruits brought directly from the fields; this is where tomatoes are packaged after being turned into ketchup or paste, and where fruits are canned to become fruit cocktail.

I came from a world bordered by limitations, primarily financial ones. Fortunately, as a child, I occupied myself with something that did not require any *dinero*, or money, because it was free. No one knew about my special hobby because I did not talk about it. Fueled by the scenes of *Star Trek*, I spent my time looking up at the sky, especially at night. At the time, I did not know exactly what had me mesmerized, but there was something up in the sky, or *cielo*, that had me fascinated. I spent hours in my bedroom, gazing through the window and staring up at the stars. I stared at *las estrellas*, or the stars, thinking: *Those stars over there are twinkling and that one over there is not. Those over there look yellow, while those over there look blue. All of them appear to be the same, but they are all so different.*

It was a magical moment when I was lucky enough to see a shooting star cross the night sky. The sight was so amazing that I would go around my neighborhood the next morning to look for the place I thought the star might have fallen.

I became oblivious to time. When I would finally fall asleep, it was to images of stars still latent in my mind. Sleep was something that I did not get much of on Friday nights because I would go to bed late and wake up early for a long weekend of work.

"Come on, wake up! We have to go work," my father would say when he would wake us every Saturday morning. If we were running late, my mother—who was young and energetic at the time—would yell, "Let's go! We're going to be late. It's already past five in the morning!" *Mamá* also took the time to gather the tools we would need to work in the fields, and she even packed our lunches, which usually consisted of tacos.

The workload in *los campos* was extremely heavy, especially for children, but my siblings and I did not mind. We enjoyed it because we knew that we were going to get paid at the end of the day. My parents let us spend a small portion of our money on *dulces y juguetes*, candy and toys, although most of our money went straight into the family savings. My family and I have always been very close and supportive of one another. As we each succeeded in life, we looked out for one another and made sure we were all improving together.

It was May and cucumber season, or *la temporada de pepinos*, in Stockton. The rows, or *surcos*, in the fields were wet and there was mud everywhere. I remember seeing the other field-workers dressed in their bandanas, straw hats, Levi's, and plaid flannel shirts. Each of us was paid fifty cents for each bucket we filled with *pepinos*, or cucumbers, that we dumped into the large wooden boxes at the end of every other ten or so rows. As I grew older, I would learn the *mañas*, or bad habits, of the other workers; this included bending the bottom of their metal buckets inward to create less volume and thus appear to fill each bucket even more quickly. I would also learn how to swiftly reseat a bucket of *pepinos* to make it look full when it really was not. "All tricks of the trade," I told myself. This was how we Hernández kids spent our weekends and summers. We knew what it was our responsibility to do and there was no way of getting around that. Every morning spent in the fields promised us the same routine of going to and fro, picking the fruits, or vegetables, from the ground as the rays of the hot sun hit our backs.

During one Saturday in particular, I fell over after accidently stepping on a yellow overgrown *pepino* that was rotten. I remember its rotten stench as I threw down my bucket, standing there thinking, "I'm all covered in mud. I stink, I'm tired, and I'm sunburned. My siblings can continue working alongside my parents but I'm not going to anymore. I want to go home to watch TV and play."

I decided to quit. I went to my father and pulled on his pant leg to tell him, "Dad, I'm tired. I want to go home!"

When he heard what I told him, he leaned down, took hold of both my shoulders, and, with a surprised look on his face, asked, "What's wrong? Did something happen? Are you okay?"

"Look at me! I'm dirty. I fell in the mud. I want to leave. Plus, I've already made ten dollars for the day," I cried to him.

"The day is almost over. Just keep on working."

"I don't want to!"

"Fine. Take a good look at yourself. You don't like what you see now, right? You don't like working the fields in the hot sun or getting dirty. Am I right? Well, if you quit now, you'll be creating a pattern that is easy to conform to. If you don't work hard in school, or in life, this will be your future. Is that what you want?"

"No," I answered him.

"Well then, don't settle for ten dollars. The day is almost over: get back to work," he ordered, with just the right balance of authority and his version of tough love.

What my father told me that day in the fields changed the

trajectory of my life. It turned into the speech that transcended the end of a long day of working in the fields. We would hear it when all four of us sat in the backseat of our ramshackle car. Father would turn around to look at us before he would turn the engine on, and he would say, "So how do you guys feel right now?" We, of course, were tired, sweaty, covered with mud, and would answer accordingly. "Good," he would say, "because you kids have the privilege of living your future right now."

"Living our future right now?" we would ask curiously.

"Yes. I am not going to force you to go to school or get good grades. But if you don't, this is the type of job you'll have for the rest of your life. This is the future that awaits you. So if you want to quit school right now, no problem; I invite you to start coming to work with me *every day* as of tomorrow!"

My father's words made me realize that if I continued going to school, I could do whatever it was I wanted to do in life. If I studied hard, I might one day make enough money so my parents would no longer have to work in the fields! To this day, I believe that my father's words changed the course of my destiny, and I am so grateful to him for that.

Soon another yearly tradition approached. In November 1968, my family and I packed all of our belongings and prepared for the drive from Stockton to my parents' hometown of La Piedad in Mexico. The journey would last more than two days, so it was necessary to pack our car with plenty of food, clothes, and blankets. Whenever my parents took us back to Mexico for the winter, they made sure we each asked our *maestra*, or teacher, for our homework so we would not fall too far behind in our schoolwork. My teacher always prepared three to four months of homework since I would not return until the following spring, around the month of February. The situation was the same for Chavita, Lety, and Gil. We felt fortunate that our teachers already knew our yearly routine.

"Ms. Johnson, can I get my homework, please? I'm going back to Mexico," I said in my broken English, as I was leaving my first grade class.

"Of course, José. Here you go."

Once I had my homework, I grabbed my personal belongings from my *pupitre*, or desk, and rushed home.

"Are we ready?"

"Yes, Dad," answered Gil, as he finished putting his book away in his backpack.

"Are we missing anything?" inquired my father.

"No. We're just waiting for Pepito to finish getting ready."

"Where is he?"

"In our room."

My father came into the bedroom and found me looking out the window. He asked me, "Everything all right, son?"

"Yes, I'm just looking at that cloud. It's shaped like a..."

He started laughing and said, "Oh son, you're looking at clouds while we're waiting for you. Come on, hurry up! Mexico is waiting for us!" And as soon as he finished telling me to hurry, he walked out of the room.

"It's shaped like a rocket," I said to myself, alone in my room.

Once I was outside, I saw that my family and our belongings were packed inside our 1965 Mercury Monterey, which was the same color as the blue sky. This trip to La Piedad was one of many that I remember clearly.

Although the road ahead of us seemed endless, just like the night sky above, there was not much farther left to go by day two. I could not fall asleep; perhaps it was due to the excitement of being within hours of waking surrounded by our loved ones in Michoacán. As the evening approached, I asked many questions, to the point of exhausting both my siblings and my father. My mother told me not to get discouraged because she similarly had ideas, questions, and doubts about things—which no one around her could answer or solve—when she was young. She continued by saying that is why one goes to school, to find the answers to such looming questions.

I attempted to close my eyes in the hope of falling asleep on several occasions, but I never entered a state of slumber because I was too focused on the stars above. An endless trail of questions wound through my mind: *I wonder how far they really are from me? They look like little lights. What's their purpose? Are they just for decoration? Why can I only see them at night?* That night there was a *luna llena*, or full moon, which followed me down the highway, never once losing sight of me. I did not take my eyes off of my new friend until I finally fell asleep.

I was eager to see the rest of my family back in Mexico. My cousins, or *primos*, and I would play together until the sun went down and the stars appeared in the night sky; they had the same skin color and dark features as me. I most looked forward to *Navidad y el Año Nuevo*, Christmas and New Year, because it was then that our extended family gathered at my grandparents' house.

I spent my days running around between the *pueblo*, or town, of La Piedad, where *mis abuelos* from my father's side lived, and *el rancho* of Ticuítaco, where *mi abuelita* from my mother's side lived. The towns were only ten minutes away from each other by bus or car; the *camión El Ranchero* would take me on my way. The *Ranchero* was the newer version of the bus my father used to drive as a young boy. Ticuítaco was very rural, surrounded by vast open land where fishing in the dam and hunting doves, or *guilotas*, were favorite pastimes. Alternatively, La Piedad was a small town that now had some cafés located around its plaza; the center of the plaza had remained marked by a kiosk—the same kiosk where my parents met and fell in love. Despite their differences, the two towns shared a commonality: both offered *paz y quietud*, peace and quiet. Additionally, the smell of the local herbs and fruits mixed together with the sound of the local music created a synergy unique to the two communities, filling the air with a rich cultural history.

Many of the locals from La Piedad traveled to *los Estados Unidos*, or the United States, in search of good fortune that comes in the form of the green of the U.S. dollar. For some, this dream became a reality and their families were even able to build modest homes.

This was La Piedad: a town of migrants, or *migrantes*, who did not have much with which to occupy themselves. *Las calles*, or the streets, were empty by eight at night, and the major attraction was the town square, affectionately known as *la plaza*. *La plaza* was where families would get together on the weekends to have coffee or ice cream; it was also where they would gather to go to Mass, or *misa*, at the *iglesia del Señor de la Piedad*. Folks say that during the time leading up to Mexico's independence, *el cura*, or the priest Miguel Hidalgo

y Costilla—a leader of the Mexican War of Independence—
often visited the church because the pastor was one of his
relatives. I remain intrigued by this historical anecdote.

When we finally arrived in La Piedad, *mis abuelos* welcomed
us with open arms.

"They're here!" shouted my paternal grandmother, Cleotilde. "My son and his family are here."

"How are you, Doña Cleotilde?" my mother asked when
she saw her.

"Good. Look at my grandchildren; they're all grown
up now!"

"Yes, they are. Time flies."

"Come, come inside. I made *tamales* and *champurradito* for
breakfast," said my *abuelita* as she led everyone inside. *Tamales*
are made of corn dough, or masa, and they are stuffed with
meat, fruit, or spices; they take a good deal of time to prepare,
as they are wrapped in banana leaf or corn husk before being
steamed in a huge pot. *Champurradito*, on the other hand, is a
delicious hot chocolate that is thickened with a bit of cornmeal.

To me, one of the most important streets in town was Pedro
Aceves; the address number 387 marked the dwelling where
my paternal grandparents lived. The outside porch was wide,
and the house was made of *adobe*. It consisted of a few bed-
rooms, a kitchen, and a bathroom. The roof was made of *teja*,
a type of curved ceramic interwoven tile. Even though their
house had an austere exterior, the interior was full of a family's
love, the same type that existed in our own home. Now that I
have a family of my own, I can share what I learned in both my
grandparents' and parents' homes with my wife and children.

When my *abuelo* José was not busy tending to his plot of

land near Ticuítaco, he would buy *molcajetes* and *metates*—both of which are made of lava rock—from the Tarascan Indians. My *abuela* used the *molcajete* to grind roasted chiles and tomatoes into a tasty salsa, and she used the *metate* to grind corn into a masa paste for tortillas. She would also occasionally use the *metate* to grind cocoa beans with sugar to make chocolate tablets for our hot chocolate. My *abuelo* would buy *molcajetes* and *metates* in bulk, and then I would help him load them onto the bus. We would then take a *viaje*, or trip, to the towns surrounding La Piedad to resell the items to the owners of stores in the *mercado*, or market. This is how I was able to see the beautiful countryside of the state of Michoacán. When we would finish for the day and return to La Piedad, my *abuelo* would give me five *pesos*. This was just enough *dinero* for me to buy a soda and a sandwich known as a *torta*.

I have fond memories of La Piedad and Ticuítaco. I spent wonderful moments playing both with my siblings, or *hermanos*, and my cousins. We spent hours on the soccer field, on the basketball court, swimming in *las albercas de "la quinta,"* or the community swimming pool, and walking the rural paths of the town. There is a beautiful dam in Ticuítaco that I believe harnesses the power to impress any soul. When the sun sets, a tint of gold is reflected in the water; this, in turn, creates what appear to be little sparkles that shimmer along the horizon like miniature magical stars.

"Look, Lety! Aren't they pretty?" I would ask my sister whenever I saw them.

"Yes, Pepe. They are," Lety would reply. "We should get home before it gets dark. *Mamá* and *Papá* are probably wondering where we are."

"You're right. Hey, Lety..."

"What?"

"Have you ever wondered what it would be like to be near to the stars and the moon?" I asked her out of curiosity.

"Why would I want to be close to them when I can see them perfectly well from here?"

"I know, but wouldn't you like to be right next to them? Do you ever think about how the stars would look up close? What would it be like to pass straight through a cloud, or to look at the sun from a place where it appears to be much bigger than it looks like it is from here?"

"Not really. I would imagine passing through a cloud is the same as driving through the fog. I don't know how you come up with these things, Pepito. Hurry up, come on! Let's go home!"

The *juegos*, or games, I played with as a child were different than the ones kids usually played with in the United States. In Mexico, the kids lacked toys and we often used our imagination to keep us entertained. I would get together with the other kids from the block on a regular basis. We would spend our afternoons *abajo*, or below, my paternal grandparents' house in La Piedad, as their house was located on a hill. Here, we would also talk about conquering the mountain next to La Piedad, which the locals knew as *el Cerro Grande*, or the Big Hill. As I grew older, I did indeed conquer—more than once—this *cerro*; I would go there to meditate, and the place served as a safe haven where I could reflect on whatever was on my mind.

While in Mexico, I spent my mornings doing my homework. After lunch, I would go to the town plaza to *La Micho-acána* for some ice cream, or *helado*. I would sit there with my *helado*, daydreaming about what the future had in store for me.

"Look, there's Pepe. Come on, let's go sit over there with him!" said Gil to Chavita and Lety.

Gil was referring to the sidewalk that was on the outskirts of the *portal Morelos*, which was where we would watch young couples drive by listening to the latest *música norteamericana*, or American music.

"When I'm older, I want a truck like that one," said Chavita, pointing at a white truck with a flame design on both sides of it as it passed by.

"That truck is really ugly! What about that red one that's coming?" asked Gil.

"No. That one is ugly too," said Lety so she would not be left out of the conversation.

"What do girls know about trucks? They only know about dolls and boys."

"That is not true, Gil!"

"Yes, it is. You're going to have a boyfriend and you're going to hold hands and kiss," said Gil in a mocking tone.

I intervened by saying, "All right, that's enough! Leave her alone. What we should be talking about is if anyone here knows what they're going to get for Christmas."

*Navidad* was the only time the whole Hernández family got together at my paternal grandparents' house. Family members would enjoy my grandmother's *pozole*, a traditional Mexican stew made of pork and hominy. The kids would break the *piñatas* that my grandfather José made. Everyone in town knew my grandfather by the nickname of Espinazo because he was tall and very slim.

My father and my grandfather José would go to the *mercado* early in the morning to buy everything *Mamá* and my *abuelita* needed to prepare our Christmas dinner: corn, tortillas, chicken, pork, and more. Meanwhile, the rest of us helped my mother and grandmother Cleotilde make the *tamales*. We also had traditional sweet drinks to celebrate *el nacimiento del Niño Dios*, or the birth of Christ. For that special moment, we partook in a *posada*, which is a nine-day procession that ends on Christmas. We paraded down the street posing as pilgrims and asking for a host family to give us a place to stay. It was so much fun because we lit candles and sang songs as we circled the neighborhood. On Christmas, we drank fruit punch and exchanged gifts before dinner.

What truly mattered to me was that I got to see many of my extended relatives who were coming from the U.S.; Mexico City, the capital of Mexico; and Villahermosa, the capital of the state of Tabasco. This would be one of the few times of the year that we were reunited. I got to see my aunts, uncles, and cousins. That was nice! Christmas not only proved to be a celebratory event for the adults, but also for us *niños*. All of us children were excited because this was the only time of the year when we got to stay up and play with our toys all night.

"Pepe!" said my *abuelo* José.

"*Sí, Abuelo,*" I responded.

"Are you having a good time?" he asked.

"Yes. Look at how much candy I got from the *piñata*," I answered with joy.

"You got a lot. May I have one?" he requested.

I sat on his lap and handed him a piece of candy.

"I can tell you're going to be a very intelligent young man," he declared.

"I don't think so. I have a hard time learning English and I don't really learn anything in school," I confessed to him.

"It's not as hard as you think. Don't give up. If you work hard, you can achieve anything in life. Believe me." He took a moment to gather his thoughts. "Do you know why they named you José?" he asked me.

"Because they wanted to name me after you?"

"Yes. And do you know who José was?"

"No," I told him.

"He was a humble carpenter who raised Jesus Christ. And do you know what a carpenter does?"

"Nope."

"It's someone who can create and shape something beautiful from a block of nothing. That is why the individuals who are named José are known as creators. You have the power to create a reality out of your dreams and shape your life accordingly."

There was nothing I loved more than listening to my *abuelo* José. He once told me that the stars above guided explorers to their final destinations when they got lost. "Why do you think people wish upon a star?" he asked me.

"I don't know," I answered.

"Because they make wishes come true! There will always be one star in the sky that will grab your attention; wish upon that star. It will be the brightest, biggest, and most beautiful star of them all."

Our time in Mexico would come to an end, and soon the car

would have to be loaded up again to turn around and head back to the U.S. Two days later, there we were again, entering the perfectly paved roads and highways of the United States. Highway 99, which took us to the Central Valley, had not changed a bit. Our neighborhoods remained the same. This time we arrived in Tracy. I went back to elementary school, or *la escuela*, the following spring. Things started to change for the better as my comprehension of the English language began to improve, little by little. I started to see that making a little extra effort in learning the language could pay off soon. I began to realize the importance of going to school and paying attention.

I vividly recall one of those days where we had to walk on a dirt road until it reached the main road. This was where we would get on the yellow *camión* that would take us to school. We sat down on the sidewalk to wait.

"Look, Lety," said Chava. "My jeans are ripped at the knee."

"Duh! You wear them to play outside. They're for school," she replied.

"My shoes are ripped on the side too."

"You're going to have to wait until *Mamá* and *Papá* can buy you new ones," Lety told him.

"Why?"

"Because they don't have any money right now."

"How do you know that?" asked Gil.

"I heard *Papá* telling *Mamá* the other day that he had very little money."

I intervened in their conversation by telling them that we had to go to school if we did not want to worry about money in the future, something our father told us constantly.

Soon after, *el camión amarillo* picked us up. No one said a single word on the subject afterward. Years later, my siblings confessed that they could not believe that their youngest sibling was the one who stood up and so seriously defended the importance of getting an education. In reality, I was not as serious as they thought I was. The only reason I strived to do well in school was because of the love I had for my parents.

Things at school continued to get better. Making friends became easier and speaking *inglés* became less of a challenge as time passed. I did not consider myself fluent in the language until the age of twelve. On the other hand, mathematics never gave me any problems. I found refuge and solace in numbers when other things seemed not to go my way. In fact, I excelled in this subject without trying.

I had my daily routine down and I followed it as strictly as a soldier would. Every day after school, I would do my homework, watch TV, and then play outside. The only things that differed from day to day were the questions that invaded my mind. I made it my personal mission to track down the answers to every single query that popped into my thoughts, constantly pursing knowledge while satisfying my curiosity.

My classmates and I counted the days of class left before summer vacation, or *las vacaciones del verano*. The majority of the kids I went to school with spent their summer vacation with family, traveling, and playing outdoors. I, on the other hand, did not have the luxury of doing any of that.

"Only three more days until summer vacation!" I heard a fellow classmate yell out with excitement.

"Well, I'll be working when you'll be playing," I told him from across the classroom.

"What? Why?"

"Because me and my whole family have to help my father by working in *los campos*."

For those growing up in my household, the word *summer* was synonymous with the word *work*. My siblings and I became accustomed to working every summer. We worked in the fields and had no time to rest or play.

The last day of class at Fillmore Elementary School in Stockton was chaotic. As soon as the bell rang to signal the start of summer vacation, every student in the school ran to the door, out of the classroom, and straight home. I was the only one who did not. My teacher, *la señorita* Young, was a young Chinese woman who taught a combined class of first and second graders. She had also taught Chava, Gil, and Lety before me. It was she who noticed how I had managed to excel in school, specifically in math.

"Shouldn't you be excited like everyone else that school is over?" she asked as she walked up to me.

"I guess," I replied, as I finished putting the rest of my stuff in my backpack.

"You're going to be working this summer, am I correct?"

"Yes."

"Well, just don't forget that school is your first priority. Have some fun this summer too. I'll see you back here when school starts."

I took my backpack, swung it across my back, and started walking away with a melancholic smile on my face when *la señorita* Young called out, "José."

I turned around.

"I just want you to know that you're a very smart boy," she told me. I looked at her with doubt in my eyes and a strong sense of pride that outweighed the humbleness that my parents instilled in me.

"Don't ever quit school to work in the fields. You have the potential to be someone important one day."

The thought of quitting school had never entered my mind. My parents, who only had a third grade education, encouraged all four of us to become professionals and focus on careers that would keep us from having to work in the fields under the hot sun. My parents' purpose for making us work in the fields was not because they needed our labor, nor was it for money; they made us literally feel the struggle of physical labor, hoping we would understand the importance of striving for *un futuro mejor*, or a better future.

Later that day, Gil entered through the front door of the house screaming, "*Mamá*, we're home! We're finally on vacation!"

"Yes, I know," she responded, even as thrilled as Gil was to be on vacation.

"But we're going to have to work in the fields all summer, right?"

"Yes, Gil. But you'll be done by noon on most days and you'll have the rest of your afternoons to yourself. Why the long face?" she wondered. "This is not going to be forever, because when you're a lawyer, doctor, or engineer—just think! You'll have your own office, and you'll go to work dressed in a suit. Then the fields will be a thing of the past," she assured him.

My family spent the months of June, July, and August working under the scorching California sun. Each day consisted of the same thing: *trabajo*, or work. I did not want my future to be in the furrows. I plowed because I wanted more out of life. I wanted to do something significant for myself, for my family, but most important, for my mother, who was always cleaning and working. She was the one who had to sacrifice all her life for the sake of her children and husband—we have always been the center of her existence. It was not easy running a household and raising four children in a foreign country. My admiration of both her strength and the extent of her sacrifice are why I did everything I could to be *un niño bueno*, a good boy.

Chava, Lety, and Gil followed my example of doing things on my own to lessen my mother's workload. In a sense, we grew up and matured faster than other kids because of the responsibilities thrust upon us early in life. Our initiative allowed Mother to rest a bit or work on other things. It kept her from having to worry about waking us up in the morning, getting us dressed, and taking us to school; these are tasks that present challenges daily in other households, let alone ones with fixed resources where every minute of time is all the more valuable. Once we got home from school, my siblings and I would start our *quehaceres* without being asked. We made our beds, cleaned our rooms, took the trash out, and mowed the lawn.

Not being in school was tiring, so I looked forward to the first day of classes. I could not wait to begin second grade; I was anxious for school to start because it would save me from having to work in the fields. However, my father's wise words gave me the strength and ability to continue looking forward. He taught me that I had to fight for what I believed in and wanted out of life. "Nothing comes to fruition without hard work and perseverance," Father would remind me. That is why I found a way to positively use my fieldwork to motivate me to succeed. As I would place each fruit I picked in my bucket—whether it was a strawberry, or *fresa*, I picked, or a peach, or *durazno*, I pulled from a tree—I would do so in exchange for a new, positive idea. With time, I had developed and thought through many ideas, helping me chart a pathway to my future. It was during that particular summer of 1969 when a major event occurred that would make a big difference in my life.

Despite the war in Vietnam, the internal conflicts in the U.S., and the hippie movement, it was an important year for humanity; it was a year that left a strong impression on me at the tender age of seven. On the morning of July 20, 1969, the entire world was glued to the television set, waiting in awe for an historic event to take place. Mankind had managed to do the unthinkable: a person was about to set foot on the Moon.

Since the beginning of time, *la luna*, or the Moon, has inspired people to write music and poetry. But, on this day, it was about to be conquered by an individual who not only took his dreams, or *sueños*, with him on his journey, but also those of every individual on Earth. Upon bearing witness to this monumental event, each person should have realized his or her possibility to dream without limitations. I know that I was inspired by the prospect of believing in something bigger than myself.

The news that circulated around the world was incredible: NASA had sent a man to the Moon! After coming home from a long day of work in the fields, my family gathered around our television set to witness mankind's first steps on the Moon. I got closer to the television to hear Walter Cronkite's narration of the unfolding event.

"*Mamá! Papá!* Hurry up! Come here!" I screamed from our living room.

"We're coming!" they responded from the kitchen where my mother was preparing dinner.

As always, I stood at my post on the side of the television to adjust the rabbit ear antenna, but this time I tried extra hard to stand still and get a good signal. I did not take my eyes off the images; I was utterly awestruck. The landing on the Moon reminded me of *Star Trek* and the science fiction films I enjoyed. The only difference now was that it was real! My siblings were compassionate, rotating spots with me at my antenna post so that I also had the opportunity to sit down and enjoy the moment. I did not blink for one second while sitting on the wooden floor in front of the TV. *Whose idea was it to send someone into space? How did they do it?* My mind wondered as I heard: "Houston, Tranquility Base here. The Eagle has landed."

Later that night, the first images of Neil Armstrong on the surface of *la luna* were transmitted into households around the globe. When he put his foot on the Moon, he uttered the famous line that has transcended time: "That's one small step for man, one giant leap for mankind." When I heard these words, I felt indescribably shocked. I was captivated by this man, by this science, which left me in awe. Absorbed in the broadcast, I got up abruptly to get closer to the television screen. I had an epiphany. During that exact moment, I discovered what

I wanted to be when I grew up: an astronaut, or *un astronauta*. And from that moment on, I was determined that absolutely nothing would get in the way of my dream.

I was only seven years old, and I did not know what being an astronaut entailed. No matter. I like to think that it was more of a predestined moment of realization rather than a silly thought that had randomly entered my mind. Just thinking about the endless universe that left so much to be discovered, my heart ached. I imagined being able to fly higher than any bird and being able to answer all of the questions about the cosmos that consumed my thoughts. I genuinely wanted to be an astronaut.

I will never forget how I felt that night when I went to bed. I was too excited to fall asleep. I could not stop thinking about my *sueño* of becoming *un astronauta*. The thought of being able to integrate science fiction with scientific reality was alluring. The thought of being able to do that while becoming someone—like Neil Armstrong—who would not only achieve success, but who would also inspire others to do the same, was overpowering. I was amazed by Armstrong's story, and I could only hope that I would one day know how it felt to wear a glass space helmet and a white space suit like he did when he so gallantly served his country.

I thought it was best not to say anything about wanting to be an astronaut, out of fear of what people would say or think. I was scared that people would laugh at me and try to break me down, so I decided that I did not want to give others the power to diminish *my* dream. The only people I did share this dream with were my parents and, to my pleasant surprise, they offered me words of encouragement. My father sat me down at the same kitchen table where my mother made us do our homework every day and offered me a few words of advice. He said if I followed his recipe, I could do anything that I wanted to when I grew up because we lived in the United States. He explained to me that my siblings and I had the opportunity to live the American Dream.

Looking at me very seriously, he said, "First, identify what you want to be when you grow up. Second, know how far you are from your goal. Third, draw yourself a road map that gives you all the steps it will take to get there. Fourth, get yourself a good education. Fifth and finally, apply the same work ethic that you have in your work in the fields to your books, and subsequently to your job once you graduate from college. Mix all this together, José, and you can be successful at anything you want to do, including becoming an astronaut!" I remember going to bed so happy that night because my parents believed I could become an astronaut—because my parents believed in me! Their support made me adamant that I could be successful in achieving my dream.

The next morning, my family and I continued filling crates with strawberries. As I picked *frutas y verduras*, or fruits and vegetables, from the ground, I dreamt of the day I would reach the stars. I was now motivated to aim high and reach my full potential. Until then, I would keep my dream quiet for many, many years...

The month of September arrived and so did the start of the second grade at Fillmore Elementary School in Stockton. I arrived at school very early—before anyone else—because I had a plan.

I learned that *la señorita* Young would be my teacher again. I went looking for her because I wanted to talk to her in private.

"José, you're back! I'm so glad to see you," she said as soon as she saw me.

"Me too."

"How was your summer?" she asked.

"Good. I worked in the fields and made some money. Most of it went to my parents and I put a little into my piggy bank," I told her.

"That's good. Did you have time to play and enjoy yourself?"

"Yes. I played with my brothers. Oh, I have something to tell you!"

"What?" said *la señorita* Young.

"I got a magazine about astronauts after I saw the launch of the Apollo on TV. I read about what they do, about space, and about the universe. I think it's all very interesting. Don't you?"

"Wow, José. I didn't know you were interested in this kind of stuff," she said, before she walked away to retrieve a book from her desk.

"This is an astronomy book," she said as she handed it to me. "I know it's old, but I think you'll enjoy it." I could not believe I was holding a book, or *un libro*, that had all the answers to my numerous questions about outer space, or *el espacio*.

"Is this for me?" I asked with some anxiety. I wanted to vivaciously read through those pages, then and there; I wanted to quell my uncertainties about space with the very answers that were now at my fingertips.

"Yes, José. It's for you to read whenever you want. And if you have any questions, ask me."

"I will. Thank you!" I said with an enormous smile on my face.

I read my astronomy book every afternoon while sitting on the edge of the bed I shared with Gil. I soon found out why the stars were distinct shades of color, why some would shine brighter than others, and why some twinkled while others did not. I learned about the constellations and what made up the universe, or *universo*. I read about Galileo Galilei and his theories, even though I did not fully understand what they meant at the time. The more I read, the more questions and doubts were eliminated from my mind, which helped to make room for new ones!

Before I knew it, fall had arrived; my family would soon be getting ready to go back to La Piedad. Once again, I asked *la señorita* Young for my homework—just like I had done the year before—but she did not want to give it to me.

"José, I'm going to come to your house tonight to speak with your parents. I want to talk to them about your trips to Mexico."

"Why? Is there something wrong?" I asked worriedly.

"I think they need to put your education first, and these frequent trips back to Mexico every year are hurting you rather than helping you. I'm really concerned," she said in a serious tone.

I knew perfectly well what *la señorita* Young was referring to, and I agreed with her. I did not want to spend another year splitting my time between living in the U.S. for the first part of the year and in Mexico for the second part. My desire was to plant my roots in one single spot to grow as a person— intellectually, socially, and emotionally. I wanted to attend only one school, even though I had not yet been able to fully master English. Admittedly, this did occasionally make me feel alienated and self-conscious.

As I walked home that afternoon, I realized the importance of having *la señorita* Young speak to my parents. She was the daughter of Chinese immigrants, but she managed to go to college and become a working professional. I think that *un inmigrante*, or an immigrant, regardless of his or her origin, tends to face difficulties assimilating to his or her new environment, making the quest for prosperity even more overwhelming.

"*Mamá y Papá!* My teacher is coming to talk to you," I told them as soon as I arrived home. My father and mother reacted differently to my news. My father immediately removed his belt, asking me why I misbehaved at school. After some fast talking, I managed to convince him that her visit was related to our upcoming trip to Mexico.

"We need to clean the house, make fresh flour tortillas, and prepare a delicious meal. When is she coming?" responded my mother, who was already beginning to fret about the arrival of our important guest.

"She said she would be here at seven o'clock."

"Well, I better hurry up and get started!" she said as she hurried to make the house presentable.

My mother, like many Mexican women, was accustomed to making sure that her guests, or *visitas,* were well attended to during their visit. But on this occasion, it was not just any guest: it was my teacher! The fact that she wanted to have a serious conversation with my parents about my education made it even more important. It was not long before I heard someone knocking on the door.

*"Maestra, qué gusto que nos visite, pase por favor,"* said my father, Salvador.

"My father says it's nice of you to visit us, and please come in," I translated.

*"Muchas gracias,"* said *señorita* Young in the little Spanish she knew.

*"Tome asiento."*

"Please, have a seat," I told her.

*"Gracias."*

She did not speak any Spanish; she only knew how to say *"sí,"* or "yes," and *"muchas gracias,"* or "thank you." Therefore, I had to translate what my father said to her in the little English I knew at the time.

*"La señorita* Young said that it's important that we stop traveling back and forth from California to Mexico because she does not want it to continue to hurt my education," I said to my father.

"My father said that we have no other choice because there is no work here during the winter, which means there's no money to live on," I told *la señorita* Young.

*"Papá,* she said that you have to view us—your children— like trees. In other words, think about what happens when you keep transplanting trees. They don't grow big and strong because they don't have a chance to grow deep roots. Kids are like trees, and this is why you need to stay in one place if you

want to give us a chance to do well in school and make something of ourselves.

"My father said that he'll be more than happy to stay here during the winter if he is able to find work.

"She said that it's important that you do everything in your power to find work here during the winter because the only way we'll be able to secure a good future is if we stop missing school so much.

"My dad said you're right and that he'll do everything he can to find work here during the winters.

"She said that it will be for the best in the end."

*"Ya está lista la cena,"* announced my mother.

"My mother said that dinner is ready," I turned to say to *la señorita* Young.

That night, during dinner, my family shared many laughs with her. We even taught her some phrases in Spanish. I could tell she enjoyed my mother's refried beans, handmade tortillas, Mexican rice, chicken mole, and *agua de horchata*—a Mexican rice drink.

After getting to enjoy an especially delicious dinner, I joked with my teacher by asking her to come to visit more often. Everybody had a nice laugh over the comment with the exception of my serious father; he shot me one of those looks that parents give their children when they are infuriated but cannot do anything because company is present. *La señorita* Young later told me how much she admired my family's hospitality and our kindness. She knew we did not live in a luxurious place, but we tried to make up for it with the great amount of gratitude and respect that we had for her.

When she left that night, she smiled, leaned down toward

me, and said, "You have a wonderful family. And don't ever give up on your dreams, because they will come true one day."

"I won't. See you tomorrow in class. *Buenas noches.*"

"Good night. *Gracias.*"

We still went to Mexico that year but we returned straight to Stockton. Our subsequent trips got shorter as we gradually started to spend the winters in Stockton. During these long winters, we lived off the little money that was saved from that year's harvest season, or *cosecha*. Our financial situation usually got worse toward the end of winter as my father struggled to find employment as a tree pruner. Winters in the United States proved to be a hardship on all of us.

"Julia, we have to limit our spending because pretty soon we are not going to have any money left for anything, not even food," my father told my mother in a worried voice.

"I know, Salvador. But don't worry. We'll get through this, even if we have to eat beans for every meal."

"It'll only be until I find work again," my father assured her.

"Like I've said, God is not going to abandon us. This is a sacrifice but it'll pay off in the end because it's for our children's future."

The winters that followed were no different. Our situation did improve a bit each year, but not by much. My father did everything he could on his part to find a solution to our money problems. He left the house each morning before the sun rose. He managed to find little day jobs, or *trabajitos*, that did not pay much. Despite our economic stress, there was always food on the table and plenty of love in our house.

I would go outside and play in the streets with the other kids from our neighborhood. Those kids had a tendency to analyze what I wore and then criticize me for it. My old T-shirts, high-water jeans, mended socks, and torn tennis shoes did not do me justice. I was always happy growing up, which is why I did not let their criticism ruin my spirit. My parents loved me unconditionally and I was close with my siblings, which was all that really mattered to me.

"Pepe, your shoes are ripped."

"I know," I said, as I kicked the ball and ran down the sidewalk, or *banqueta*.

"Is it true that your parents are poor?"

As difficult as it was to do, I knew that there were times when it was best to just stay silent and disregard the hurtful comments. Greg, one of the neighborhood kids, did not seem to care if I was rich or poor. He lived alone with his mother, who worked as a secretary at a lawyer's office. Greg seemed to have all the material things he needed and more. However, he always spent his afternoons at home, alone, since his mother worked all day and his sister had moved out.

He did everything he could to show the world that he was strong and content; although inside, he was hiding his fears and loneliness. I later learned that Greg had a difficult time making friends. He did not know how to maintain friendships, or any relationships. While his story saddened me, it helped me to realize that money is not everything; in spite of being economically challenged, I was fortunate to be blessed with such a loving family. When I understood Greg's situation, I went home to *Mamá* and gave her a big bear hug and a kiss before going straight to the kitchen to finish my homework. Greg, unfortunately, did not live past his adolescent years; he was struck with leukemia and passed at the tragically young age of sixteen.

CHAPTER 3

# Gaining Traction

*Education is the most powerful weapon which you can use to change the world.*

NELSON MANDELA (1918–)
ANTI-APARTHEID ACTIVIST, FORMER
PRESIDENT OF SOUTH AFRICA

The following spring there was a lot of work in *los campos*, which translated into income for my family. My father and the other *trabajadores*, or workers, constantly spoke about different things as they worked under the hot sun. One day, they discussed the value of having an education. The *trabajadores* soon learned that my father was a strong advocate for education, and they took note that none of his children worked in the fields during the week. The *campesinos* told my father that he should have his children working in *el campo*, especially since they were growing older and stronger, instead of letting their manpower go to waste in a classroom.

I remember one particular incident on a Friday evening when my father and his friends were out in our front yard talking and having a beer after a long week of work. Ezequiel—a fellow migrant worker who was also from La Piedad—told my dad that he had just cashed six checks because his wife and kids helped him out in the fields.

"I cashed eight checks," said another acquaintance, Jorge, as he proudly waved his check stubs in the air like a fan.

Ezequiel then added: "Salvador, you are losing out on four checks! You have four strong kids, and our future depends on how hard we work out there in the fields. Don't you want to build your house quickly in Mexico? You can earn a lot more money if you make your kids work all seven days of the week, not just on Saturdays and Sundays."

This was something my dad would hear every payday, but my father always ignored them or managed to change the conversation. He valued his convictions more than cashing a few extra checks every *quincena*, or biweekly pay period. He wanted his children to become educated adults. There was nothing anyone could do or say to make him change his mind.

"I only cashed two checks today, but I'm not worried; there's food on my table and my family has everything they need. I'm not ashamed of how we live. It may take a bit longer but I too will build my house," said my father.

"I hear you are thinking about once again staying here for the winter, Don Salvador? What were you thinking when you decided to stay here last winter when there was hardly any work?" inquired his friend Jorge, trying to understand my father's mentality.

My father smiled and casually brought up a new topic. "Who watched the moon landing?" he asked.

My parents made hard choices without having a clear idea as to whether or not their children would be inclined to seize the opportunities that had been made available. I credit my father and mother for giving my siblings and me the opportunity to get an education. When conversations on this subject took place, I was old enough to realize the sacrifices my parents were making and vowed not to let them down. There is no telling what my future would have been had my parents not made their children's education a priority. My siblings and I were some of the few lucky children with that opportunity; the majority of the kids we grew up with had no choice in how they spent their days, giving them no choice in how they could spend their futures.

Because my family's *situación económica*, or financial state, was at its worst during the winter months, my parents had to pinch pennies. The looming hardship prompted them to perpetually reexamine how they were budgeting expenses. During one of those tough years, they were not able to pay the rent on our home. This led to us moving to a *casita*, or smaller house, in a very low-income neighborhood located on the east side of Stockton.

"Is this where we're going to live?" asked my sister, Lety, when she saw the grim condition of this house. The living conditions were even more austere than at our previous home. The *casita* was an old, wooden, dilapidated structure that stood alongside two other *casitas*. The houses were squeezed together on a lot that would normally hold one house. All three *casitas* could have fallen down if someone stomped too hard—or at least that was how it seemed.

"Yes, but it will only be until we get back on our feet," my father said to reassure Lety that everything would soon be fine.

"Our other house was way better," said Gil.

"Be quiet, Gil! Don't listen to him, *Papá*," said Chavita.

"It's only going to be for a little while, right, *Papá*?" asked Gil, hoping for reassurance.

"Of course, just wait and see. This is only temporary. Now,

go and put your things in your new room so we can eat the *taquitos* your *Mamá* made."

A few years later all three houses would be condemned and demolished, one by one, by the owner. Our house was the last one left standing. The landlord chose for our house to be demolished last because he wanted our family to move into a newly installed house on the same lot. I could only assume this was the case because my father always prided himself in paying the rent on time, thus making us the best tenants.

Since the houses had been built on raised foundations, this allowed our landlord to buy a preexisting house and move it onto the lot. The landlord purchased a house in slightly better condition than any of the *casitas* had been in and had it mounted on a newly constructed elevated foundation. The new foundation left a big enough gap under the house to create a crawl space that later became a nice hiding place for the family dog, a mixed-breed German shepherd named Lobo.

After a few more years of renting, my parents would buy this house from the landlord. The landlord facilitated a rent-to-own finance plan that I—as a twelve-year-old kid—helped translate and explain to my father. Finally, the family had a place to call home, although our new *barrio*, or neighborhood, was far from ideal. It had a slew of problems, just as any other *barrio* in South and East Stockton did. Since we were in one of the older and more depressed neighborhoods, we witnessed far more crime than the people who lived in the newer part of town.

I started school at Fremont Middle School, which was located within walking distance of our house. The majority of the students, or *estudiantes*, not surprisingly came from a background similar to mine. My first day at Fremont was an exciting one. I was free to choose some of my own classes for the first time. I tended to focus more on the subjects that dealt with numbers and science because these subjects captivated me. Moreover, I felt comfortable, instead of intimidated, when learning about these subjects. Perhaps this was because English was my second language, and I found refuge in understanding that two plus three would always equal five in any language. Besides, I remained determined to make my dream of becoming an astronaut a reality, and by this time I knew being good in science and math was a must.

I started to become more social at school and in my *barrio*. It was at Fremont Middle School where I met Carlos and his older brother Alberto. Another person I hung around with in school was my friend Sergio; he lived across the street from me. The four of us became like brothers. We stuck together through our adolescent years; we were there for each other, in good times and bad times.

"Do you guys know what a *pocho* is?" asked Carlos while we were sitting on the stairs in front of my house.

"No," Sergio and I answered jointly.

"A *pocho* is a Mexican born here in the United States who is neither a Mexican nor an American, like us!" he explained.

Carlos and Sergio wore those white T-shirts without sleeves, baggy grey khaki pants, and shiny black Stacy Adams dress shoes that always looked too big for their feet. Their accessories generally consisted of a bandana—either neatly folded in their back pocket or worn around their head, covering most of the forehead—and a chain that hung from a belt loop.

"Is it a bad thing to be *pocho*?" I asked.

"No. But in case you haven't noticed, they don't seem to like us here in the U.S. or in Mexico. They will pick on us here or there. That's why we have to stick together. If we don't, we'll be easy targets and they'll get us."

"Who will get us?"

"The *gringos* and the Mexicans that come straight from Mexico. As I said, they don't like us. When we go to Mexico, they tell us that we're too Americanized; meanwhile, the *gringos* call us dirty Mexicans. Either way, we can't win. It's like we have no roots and don't seem to belong in either place. I'm telling you, that's why we have to stick together."

"Because we look Mexican and speak English, we don't belong?" I asked, in my somewhat improved English.

I realized what Carlos had said was true; it seemed that I did not have any permanent roots in the U.S. or in Mexico. I was a *Mexicano* who spoke Spanglish, for which even my own extended family in La Piedad made fun of me. I felt a bit of sadness because I wanted—I needed—to belong somewhere. I suppose I attached myself to Carlos, Alberto, and Sergio because they helped me fill the void that resulted from being a *pocho*.

Things around my neighborhood were never easy. Gangs were everywhere, and they congregated on a daily basis hoping to define their territories. *Drogas* like marijuana were commonly used and sold in our *barrio*. Drive-by shootings occurred to a lesser extent but nonetheless kept the neighborhood on edge. Families were dysfunctional, divided, and grew apart due to inattentive parents suffering from alcoholism or various other addictions. The children from these broken homes were quickly recruited to join gangs, so year after year, the membership of these groups multiplied. I admit that it was difficult to escape that environment. Although I managed to steer clear of such activities, I had to somewhat assimilate in order to survive.

Soon, my appearance and attitude began to change. As I spent more time with Carlos, Alberto, and Sergio, I became tougher and tougher—or so I thought. I began wearing baggy pants, oversized flannel shirts, and shoes that were one size too big. I walked down the streets, or *calles*, with an attitude while I was emulating Alberto's gestures. My objective was to conceal the true José while trying to look like the rest of my peers. I did not want to be labeled a "schoolboy" or "bookworm" so that I could avoid being harassed. However, when I was in class and with my family, I was my true self: I was playful, studious, and responsible. But when I was on the streets, I was one of the "homeboys," as we *pochos* would call ourselves. The price of assimilation was steep; soon, I started to deny that I knew how to speak Spanish and I began paying less attention to my Mexican roots.

My friend Carlos did not have any interest in school, which was a shame because he was really smart and had a lot of potential. He regularly beat my test scores throughout the seventh grade.

"José, my brother, Alberto, is going to come pick us up right now."

"Carlos, why don't you do your homework anymore? I think if you would study more . . ."

"You sound just like my mom, José. Tell me, why should I study?"

"So you can be someone important one day," I told him.

"What? Be realistic, homey. There are no opportunities for people like you and me! We are in a country that does not belong to us, and even if we lie about not being able to speak Spanish and change our customs, the *gringos* still look down at us for being Mexican. Look at the color of our skin: it's brown. They associate it with being dirty and poor. The only future we have is in the fields and factories. It's the truth and you know it."

Carlos spoke so eloquently and seemed more mature for his age. Each one of his words and the voice in which he spoke them was a testament to his suffering. He grew up in a broken home full of violence and disillusionment. And it did not help that there was always alcohol available at his fingertips.

"You're right, but . . ."

"*Chale*, José. You'll see that in the end, studying is a waste of time," he said adamantly. "Here comes my bro. Let's go!"

Sixteen-year-old Alberto spent the majority of his time with friends, or homeboys. The girls lusted after his strong physique; in other words, he was a popular guy in the *barrio*. He had no problem fighting anyone who dared to challenge him. School was definitely not a priority for him. But when he did go to school, he would cause fights inside and outside the classroom. Not a single one of his teachers could tolerate or control him. There was nothing his parents could do to control him either; he was defiant, and their own domestic problems made it hard for them to exercise any consistent authority over him. And Alberto was more interested in doing business that earned him money than he was in school or in his parents' problems. He used his cash to buy expensive things:

leather jackets, designer shirts, and gold jewelry. He bought his brother, Carlos, anything he wanted, whenever he wanted it, especially alcohol. Alberto's best friend was Sergio. The two would always loiter around the neighborhood with their older friends, forming a loosely knit gang that was not afraid of getting into trouble. Everyone was afraid of Alberto because he was extremely reckless and he did not think about the consequences of his actions.

"Carlos, what does Alberto do that he gets so much money?" I questioned him one day.

"It's hard to explain."

"Why?" I asked, eager to know more than ever.

"José, everyone knows but they just don't say anything. They're either scared or they want what he sells."

"What does he sell?"

"This." He took out a clear plastic sandwich bag from his pocket to show me. It contained something that looked like bits and pieces of dried oregano. However, I was now old enough now to realize that what Carlos was holding was marijuana. I sighed, realizing that Alberto was one of the many drug dealers in our vicinity.

"But that stuff is bad," I told him.

"No. Says who? He doesn't force anyone to buy it."

"Yeah, but...my parents told me..."

"They told you what everyone else says, 'drugs are bad.' Nothing is bad about it, trust me," he said. He paused for a moment before continuing. "What? Are you going to snitch?" he asked, with a menacing and threatening look on his face.

"No, of course not."

Years later I wondered what I could have done to better

handle that situation. I never thought about saying anything to anyone. Just as Carlos told me: "Everyone knows but they just don't say anything." At that time, the only thing I was able to offer was good advice. I tried to be a good example, so they would see within themselves how wrong they were and what they were capable of being. Perhaps that was why Alberto and Sergio were fond of me, or maybe it was because I was an easygoing kid who listened and looked up to them. They knew I was not like the other kids, and they liked that about me. Alberto never told me what he did to get money, but I knew. Unfortunately, later in life, his drug dealings and use of drugs brought about dire consequences. We all make our own choices in life, but sometimes it is harder than we realize to make the right choice. I still wonder, to this day, if there was anything that I could have done or said to persuade my three friends from choosing the path that they ultimately followed.

As the months went by, my desire to become an astronaut grew stronger. My teachers—especially my Spanish teacher at Fremont Middle, *la señora* Silvia Bello—were well aware that I had a "hunger for knowledge." *Señora* Bello was a vibrant, petite woman with brown eyes and brown hair. Born in Puerto Rico, she immigrated to the U.S. for the same reason many people do: to seek the American Dream. She had the same mentality of getting ahead and improving one's life through knowledge as I did. There was never a day when she did not talk to me about the importance of a college education. She was the first to teach me that knowing two languages was actually an advantage, not a disadvantage. Her Spanish classes were extremely hard, but for the first time, I would learn the proper way of speaking and writing the language.

One day *señora* Bello came to class and said, "I have spoken with the principal and he has given me permission to organize a trip to Guadalajara, Jalisco, in Mexico. For those who are interested, we will go during spring break by bus, so it will take approximately two days to get there. We will stay at a school for blind children. This will allow us to see and experience Mexican culture firsthand while we practice our Spanish."

Everyone in the class was enthusiastic about the idea except me. I was worried about where the money would come from to pay my way. I raised my hand and asked, "*Señora* Bello, how exactly are we going to pay for this trip?" My parents were definitely not in the position to help me pay for it.

"Thank you for asking, José. I'm thinking about putting together two fundraisers. The first will involve all of you selling boxes of chocolates and the second involves selling food. It will cost about $225 for each student who wants to go on this trip."

Our class spent the upcoming months selling chocolate bars to our fellow classmates and neighbors while *señora* Bello sold burritos for breakfast and lunch out of her office. We soon raised enough money for everyone who signed up to go to do so without having to ask their parents for a single dime. The only thing left for us to do was to wait for spring break to arrive. We were ecstatic about heading off to Guadalajara.

The night before I left on my trip, my mother helped me pack my *maleta*, or suitcase, and my sleeping bag. When she was folding my clothes, she looked at me nostalgically.

"What's wrong?" I asked.

"This is the first time that you'll be away from home by yourself," she said as she began to tear up.

"Don't cry, *Mamá*," I said, as I gave her a hug.

"You're growing up so fast. Soon you'll be married with a family of your own, and I'll be all alone."

I did not know what to say to my mother at that point. It was one of the few times that I remained silent—I was speechless. I took my hand and started to caress her hair before I told her, "I will never leave you or *Papá*. I promise."

The next morning, my father drove me to Fremont Middle School. The chartered *camión* that would take our class to Guadalajara was scheduled to pick us up there. We waited anxiously until the *camión* finally arrived. All the students hopped on board right away, including me. We all found a seat and a buddy to pass the time with before we waved good-bye to our relatives and drove off the school premises.

I took a seat next to the window and looked back to see Stockton get smaller and smaller the farther south we headed on Highway 5. I decided to treat this as an adventure and pretend I was an explorer going to unknown lands. After all, daydreaming about different worlds was something I did regularly as a young child during my family's road trips to Mexico.

We reached the *frontera*, or U.S.-Mexico border, within the day. At that point, *señora* Bello informed us that we had to get off the *camión*. The border officials had to check our documents and perform a routine search before we would be allowed to continue driving into Mexico.

Along the way, we periodically stopped for quick stretches, bathroom breaks, and food in Tijuana, Hermosillo, Empalme, and Mazatlán. Two days after leaving Stockton, we reached our final destination: Guadalajara. Many were glad that the long bus ride was over because they were not accustomed to traveling in this way. As for me, I was full of energy because I was used to the long drives.

We were taken to a group home where blind children lived. Its façade clashed with the beautiful architecture of the surrounding buildings. Nothing could have prepared us for what we were about to encounter. The condition of the home was somber, to say the least. I felt anguish. I felt as if someone was pressing down hard on my chest. I was very emotional and sad. I did not think it was fair for the children, or *niños*, to have to be sequestered in the group home, unable to experience the outside world or live normal lives like other children their age.

The teachers and blind children welcomed us with open arms and did everything to make us feel at home given their limited resources. They made sure that the "*gringitos*" were comfortable and attended to at all times.

One of the blind students caught my attention. While all the other blind children were sitting at their respective desks and laughing at my classmates, who were attempting to speak Spanish in front of the class, he was in the corner—aloof and alone. So I went up to him and asked him his name.

"My name is José," he answered.

"Me too!" I said.

"Really? Where are you from?"

"I'm from the United States. I was born in California. Where are you from?"

"I'm from here."

"Where are your parents?" I asked him.

"I don't know. They don't visit me too much."

"Do you have any friends?"

"Not really. The people here don't speak to me very much."

"What do you do for fun?"

"Nothing. I just wait around for my parents to come visit me."

I felt an indescribable sadness when I heard him tell me that.

"Well, you now have a new friend with the same name as you."

A lot of thoughts started to run through my mind at that moment: *How would it feel to be abandoned by your own family? How would it feel to not to have anyone for support or guidance? How would it feel to go outside and not be able to see the beauty of the world? How would it feel to not be able to look up at night and see how the stars shine in the dark sky?* I patted him on the back, which brought a *sonrisa*, or smile, to his face.

One day, *la señora* Bello and the man in charge of the group home gave me permission to take José on a walk around the block.

"It's been forever since I've been outside. I can feel the breeze on my face. The sun is also shining on my face, right?"

"*Sí*," I told him.

"I lost my vision when I was young," he confessed to me, "but I still remember how the trees, the sun, and the clouds look."

"What about the stars? Do you remember how they looked?"

"Of course! I used to gaze up at them at night. My mom would tell me that everyone had their own star to wish upon."

"Can I tell you something?" I asked with confidence.

"Sure. Anything."

"One day, I'm going to reach those stars. And I'll come back and tell you how they look from up close."

"Really?"

"*Sí*," I promised.

My classmates, *señora* Bello, and I returned to Guadalajara the following year. It was clear that since we enjoyed the location and learned so much from the experience that *señora* Bello was going to make this an annual pilgrimage for her top Spanish class students. I managed to save some money throughout the year to buy some transistor radios to take with me on my second trip to give to the blind children. I bought a special and slightly more expensive radio for my friend José. When I got there, I asked for José, but nobody could tell me where he was or what had happened to him. Finally, toward the end of the weeklong trip, *señora* Bello told me that he had succumbed to the tumor that had taken his vision.

I took the radio I was going to give him and set it on the small nightstand that was next to his bed. I turned on the radio and walked away, not caring who would become its new owner. The rest of the trip was a blur. I could not stop thinking about how José might have suffered during his final days of life.

"When you go off to college, you will see that everything I tell you about the importance of going to school is true," *señora* Bello would tell us.

"I want to go to college and my *mamá* wants me to go too. She wants me to be a lawyer," I informed her.

"Do you want to be a lawyer, José?" she asked.

"No," I said honestly.

"Then what do you want to be?"

"An astronaut," I said hesitantly. *La señora* Bello was the first person outside of my family I had ever told about my dream of becoming an astronaut.

"An astronaut? Why do you want to be an astronaut?"

"Every time I go work in the fields, I look up at the sky and dream about flying higher than an airplane. I'm obsessed with the stars, and I want to see the entire universe. I know it sounds crazy, but it's true."

"No. Not at all, José. If you want to be an astronaut, and if you work hard enough and believe in yourself, then you'll be an astronaut."

"How?" I asked her. "My family is poor; they won't be able to help me pay for college. I don't want them to have to work harder in the fields just so I can go to school," I said, disillusioned.

"Well then, continue doing well in school so you can get a scholarship to pay for your college. There are always options and solutions to every problem in life; you just have to find them."

Options? Those were nonexistent in the world I came from. The only thing that existed was the notion of survival. I constantly woke up to robberies, gang violence, and even murders. Some of the crimes in my neighborhood were orchestrated by my own friends. Luckily, I was able to stay away from the horrible incidents that occurred around me. What kept me from walking down the wrong path was my parents' expectation that my siblings and I would go to college. They lived for the moments when their four children would enter professional fields of work. Their firm belief was that honesty—in and out of school—along with a willingness to work hard, or *ganas*, as they called it, would lead to our success. I now reflect upon this recipe for success—which they first shared with me when I told them of wanting to be an astronaut—and am convinced that this was what empowered me to believe in myself. My parents believed in me and this, in my own simple world, led me to believe that I could become an astronaut. In essence, with their recipe, they gave me the license to dream.

Had my parents gone to college, I know they would have made excellent psychologists. They were also excellent motivators. I remember a specific incident that tested my honesty outside of school and that showed my father's ability to motivate me to do the right thing:

"Look, *Papá*. I found a wallet."

"Whose is it, *mijo*?"

"I don't know. I haven't looked inside to see," I said as I opened it to see if I could find out to whom it belonged. I read the identification and said, "It belongs to David Stone. He lives in Oakland. It says so on his license. Wow, there's four hundred dollars in cash in here too!"

"And what are you planning to do?" inquired my father.

"Let's go to Oakland, *Papá*, so I can return it!" I said.

"Is there a phone number in there somewhere? Perhaps we can call him and have him come instead."

I looked hoping to find one, but there was nothing.

"No, *Papá*. Come on, let's go! He's probably looking all over for his wallet and money as we speak."

The thought of not returning the wallet and keeping the four hundred dollars never crossed my mind. I knew it would have helped my parents out tremendously with bills and groceries, but it was not the right thing to do. I knew my conscience would not have been the same afterward if I had not chosen the moral high ground.

My father was proud that his youngest child did the right thing and went through the trouble of returning something so valuable to its owner. I could see it on his face as he drove us to Oakland that same day. He told me *chistes*, or jokes, on the way, and though some were not funny, I would laugh as a courtesy to him. In addition, he shared with me some anecdotes from his life. One of the most emblematic conversations of my teenage years took place during the drive to return the lost wallet.

"I'm really glad that you're turning into an honest and responsible young man, Pepe," my father confessed. "Not everyone your age is like you."

"I have dreams of becoming successful and important when I'm older, *Papá*. You and *Mamá* will not have to work anymore; I'll make sure of that," I promised him.

"Thank you for being a good son, Pepe. You know something, every time you come home with your report card and show us your good grades, your *mamá* cries for joy. I ask your *mamá* what we've done to deserve such a smart son when we're just two poor *campesinos* who barely know how to read and write."

"*Ay Papá*."

"It's true. You can be anything you want to be: a lawyer, a doctor, or an engineer. Whatever you choose, we'll support you in whatever way we can."

"I'm going be an engineer, *Papá*. Watch!"

"An engineer? Wow! You're going to have to study a lot of math and science. Your brother Chava wants to be an engineer too. Both of you are very smart."

I was confident that I would not let the environment that surrounded me keep me from achieving what I set out to do. I realized that it was my responsibility to make sure that the neighborhood kids and naysayers would not influence me to do otherwise; I could not let them deter me from being all that I could be. I owed a lot to my *padres*, or parents, for sacrificing so much so my siblings and I could chase our dreams in a country that allowed people from humble beginnings to achieve their dreams.

When we finally arrived in Oakland at Mr. David Stone's house, we waited as a fifty-five-year-old man answered the door. He could not believe that someone took on the responsibility of returning his wallet.

"I can't believe this! This is my wallet," he said, shocked.

"I found it. And I saw your address on your license," I told him. "So I asked my father if we could come and return it to you."

"Thank you so much for coming all the way over here to return it to me. If you hadn't, I wouldn't have been able to pay my rent and utilities this month. I don't know what I would have done," revealed Mr. Stone.

"My son found it on his way home from school and asked me if I would drive him here to return it to you," my father said proudly.

"I thank you, gentlemen. And for you, young man, here is twenty dollars for your good deed," he said as he handed me a crisp twenty-dollar bill.

"Twenty dollars! Thank you!" I took the bill, neatly folded it in half, and put it in my pocket. He also gave my father a ten-dollar bill for gas and congratulated him on raising such a "fine young man."

This was an important lesson for me to learn: honesty does have its rewards.

Junior high school would prove to be a pivotal time for many students, including me. My classmates and I were making the most important choices of our lives with respect to the future of our education. It was clear to me that my neighborhood friends—Sergio, Alberto, and Carlos—were not going to try to obtain a high school diploma, much less a college education. On the other hand, I had been programmed by my *mamá* to believe that I had to go to college. Getting a college degree was no longer just a hope; it was an expectation.

I was blessed to have had two great teachers in junior high school who reinforced my *mamá*'s aspirations for me. The first was my math teacher, Mr. Dave Ellis. Upon taking notice of my mathematical abilities, Mr. Ellis immediately moved me up to advanced algebra and geometry classes. By the ninth grade, a small group of six students had exhausted all available math classes. He suggested the creation of a calculus class where we would get a head start in advanced high school math.

The second influential teacher was *la señora* Bello, who taught me the importance of embracing my culture and who reinforced my parents' beliefs that shortcuts in life did not exist. She and my parents believed that hard work was the key to success.

I started my freshman year of high school at Franklin High School in east Stockton. At the time, Franklin was one of the toughest schools in Stockton, with its delicate balance of Caucasian, Latino, and African American students. Perhaps what made me feel good was the fact that several teachers from Fremont Middle School were asked to transfer to Franklin Senior

High School, among them *señora* Bello and Mr. Ellis. I was also comforted by the fact that my sister, Lety, was a junior and my brother Gil was a sophomore when I started there. I remember initially hanging out with them during lunch because they provided me protection from the older students who were determined to haze the new freshmen. I found refuge in something I awkwardly called my best friend: math. Yes, math made me smile, and it was fun. It remained my strongest subject as I maintained good grades throughout my four years in high school.

"Mr. Zendejas, do you have a second?"

"Of course, José. I'm just grading exams. What's going on?"

"I really don't know a lot about the history of Mexico or where I come from. I mean, I do know some things about the Aztecs, the Mayans, and some stuff about the independence of Mexico from Spain, but I want to know more."

"José, I think it is great that you want to know more about Mexico," said Mr. Zendejas. "I think you can find who you really are in the history of your ancestors' country. I know I did. José, don't ever be ashamed of your culture and its traditions. They are what make up your identity. You should be proud of who you are. Do you know why?"

"No," I answered attentively.

"Because you belong to two countries and two cultures. And that's a wonderful thing! Not everyone is as fortunate as you are."

Mr. Zendejas, a Mexican American himself, was my history teacher. I thoroughly enjoyed how he taught history, as he told it in an almost storybook fashion and kept things interesting. I also looked up to him, since he was one of a few Latino teachers in the high school. During my senior year, he would help me write my essays for scholarships and entrance applications to the universities.

Mr. Zendejas recommended that I read some books on *la historia de México*, or the history of Mexico, which I did. I learned about the Aztecs and their dominance before the Spanish Conquest. I read how the Mayans were the great scientists of their time—with a keen interest in astronomy— and how they invented the concept of zero in mathematics. I came to know about Father Miguel Hidalgo, *la Revolución*, and *la Reforma*. There were pages upon pages describing the actions of men and women who fought with courage for Mexico's future. I stared at the pages containing José Clemente Orozco's murals that depicted those struggles, reflecting on how he seemed to bring those moments to life in his paintings. I encountered those same paintings in the government buildings of Guadalajara during our trips to Mexico with *señora* Bello.

I was starting to understand the sacrifices my ancestors had made just so later generations could enjoy the benefits of a simple concept called *freedom*. After learning of the rich history of my country of origin and the leaders who fought for it, I was proud to say that part of me belonged to that nation. After having that realization, I was no longer ashamed of eating tacos during lunch or of speaking Spanish publicly. I was proud to be a *Mexicano Americano*, a *Latino*, a *Chicano*, a *Vato*, or whatever label society wanted to brand me with. All I knew was that I had the unique opportunity to live in a bicultural environment, and I was determined to utilize the best parts of each culture to my advantage.

Time flew, but my memory never failed to record a single moment of my life, *mi vida*.

I was sixteen years old by the time I was a junior at Franklin, precisely the year elections for a new student body president took place. Whoever was elected took on the responsibility of representing the entire student body when it came time to make important decisions on various issues that would affect the school as a whole. Mrs. Felton, the student affairs teacher—who was an assertive African American woman—made an announcement one day in class: "You can sign up starting today to run for a student body officer position. Remember, you have to decide what office to run for, fill out one of the forms, and drop it off in the main office."

"When do we vote?" asked the classmate sitting behind me.

"Next month. So decide now if you're going to run because you don't have much time to campaign," advised Mrs. Felton.

The classmate sitting behind me tapped me on the shoulder and said, "I think you have what it takes, José. You should run."

*Run?* I thought. "Run for what?" I told him.

"Run for student body president. You can be *el presidente*!" he quickly replied.

Throughout the day, I thought about what my classmate had suggested and it boggled my mind. Many thoughts ran through my mind: *Should I run? Why? Would someone even vote for me? Would they vote for a Latino? Could I actually be elected student body president?* I did not know what to think or do. I found it odd that someone thought I had what it took to be a leader. I had my doubts and was even scared. After being encouraged by other classmates, I decided to go ahead and run.

After class I went to one of my favorite teachers and said, "Mr. Ellis, I want to run for student body president."

"Great! I think you'd do a great job, José!" he said. "Put a good team together and start campaigning."

I always knew that I wanted to be a leader and this was the ideal opportunity for me to prove myself. I knew perfectly well that it was not going to be easy for me as a Latino in a high school where fights over one's ethnicity were starting to be the norm. It did not help that the fights were sensationalized and characterized as riots by our local newspaper.

I campaigned during lunch by shouting: "I will work hard so things change for the best for everyone at this school."

"Vote for José Hernández for student body president," shouted my classmates who helped me campaign for votes. "Vote for change."

The other *candidatos*, or candidates, did not think I had a chance at winning the race, but they soon saw that my popularity began to grow; this was something they had not anticipated. Mysteriously, the campaign posters my team put up throughout the school started to disappear. But I was not deterred, as my friends and I quickly created new ones just about as fast as the opposition would take them down.

One day, sitting at lunch, I overheard a conversation at a table behind me of students who thought that a "beaner" should not be elected student body president. I carefully turned around so these students would not see me, but I saw that the comments came from fellow classmates who I thought were friends and supporters of my campaign. Outwardly, I remained strong; inwardly, I was hurt by the harsh words that came out of my classmates' mouths. But I knew that I had to continue on and keep fighting for what I thought was right, even if I faced resistance along the way. It was painful to think that some of my peers saw me as inferior to them. I could not believe that the phrase "we are all equal," which my father had always told me, was not a view that my own classmates held. At that moment, a piece of advice that my mother had given to me came to mind. She said that whenever I came across people who do not like me, I should "overwhelm them with love," and eventually they will realize that I am a great human being. Remembering my mother's words made me feel better.

"Are you all right?" asked *la señora* Bello when she saw me walking in the hall.

"Yes," I told her.

"Looks like something is bothering you. Is it the campaign?"

"Why are they so mean?" I asked her.

"Who? *Los gringitos*?"

"Yeah. I didn't do anything to them."

"I know, I know."

*La señora* Bello gave me a strong hug that squeezed out all of the sorrow I had locked inside, which made me even more emotional.

"José, look at me. If I didn't see the potential in you, I would tell you to quit the campaign. But you are a leader, and you have dreams. You want to be an astronaut, right?"

"Yes."

"And do you think it's going to be easy?"

I did not answer her because I did not know at the time if it was or not.

"It's not going to be. It's going to be a very hard goal to

accomplish, and the last thing you need to do is learn how to quit. Ignore whatever it is they say and move forward, because the color of your skin has nothing to do with what you are capable of doing."

After she walked away, I walked over to the *ventana*, or window, and looked up at the sky and clouds. I saw a bird fly across the sky with such vigor that it became clear to me that *señora* Bello was right: I could not give up! Those students were making negative comments about me out of their own insecurities. I was a threat in their eyes. There was no way I was going to allow them to deter me from campaigning for what I believed in.

I continued to campaign. More and more students saw my determination and they promised me their votes. The morning of the election, a rumor circulated that the election was ironically going to come down to two candidates: Tiffany Smith, an African American classmate, and me. The other candidate rested on her laurels of popularity and had not actively campaigned; thus, she was now considered the long shot.

The final hours came when every student got to cast his or her vote. After the long lines at the voting polls ceased, each ballot was counted.

Tiffany and I were both nervous. We waited anxiously for the results with our campaign teams in the classroom next door to the main office, which was where the ballots were being tallied.

"You won, José!" yelled Bertha, a friend of mine, who was one of the people representing my campaign during the vote count.

"Really? You're kidding!" I said in disbelief.

"No. I'm not. It was close, but you won," she said.

"José, you are the new student body president," I heard Mrs. Felton and Mr. Ellis say as they came forward to congratulate me.

"Thank you. I can't believe it."

Tiffany was visibly disappointed because she did not win. I remember going up to her afterward and shaking her hand. I congratulated her on a great, hard-fought campaign. As I did so, my father's words resonated in my head: *To be a man is to be humble*. This is a belief that, to this day, I still ascribe to.

*El año*, the year, 1980, was not only the start of a new decade but also the year I graduated from high school. During that year, I finalized my college plans. My family's economic situation had improved a bit, but not by much. My older siblings and my mother had made the transition from working in *los campos* to better-paying jobs at the *canerias*, or canneries. My father also started driving trucks that took these fruits and vegetables from the fields directly to the canneries.

The family was starting to live the American Dream. Chava, Lety, and Gil were already in college and preparing themselves for an even better future. When I was thirteen years old, my parents sent Chava to Michoacán to study engineering. Lety—who by age nineteen had married a man by the name of Gabriel, who was also from Michoacán—was majoring in accounting. Gil was in Tulsa, Oklahoma, studying how to assemble an airplane airframe and how to be a power plant technician. As for me, I was not exactly certain of what type of engineering degree I wanted to pursue at the university.

My childhood dream of becoming an astronaut was still in

the back of my mind. Honestly, I had doubts it would happen until, one day, I heard a news brief on the radio that said: *"Costa Rican Franklin Chang Díaz, the first Latino American astronaut candidate at NASA, makes his dream come true!"*

The news commentator talked in depth about Dr. Chang Díaz's struggles and triumphs in his quest to become an astronaut. *"Franklin Chang Díaz was born in 1950 in San José, Costa Rica. He was sent to the United States after finishing his secondary education with only fifty dollars to his name and without knowing a single word of English. He recounted that all he had was a suitcase full of aspirations."*

The commentator continued, saying: *"His family back in Costa Rica was poor and wanted him to make something of himself. He received a scholarship from the University of Connecticut, where he graduated with a degree in mechanical engineering in 1973. Four years later, he obtained his doctorate degree in nuclear engineering from Massachusetts Institute of Technology. Today, he is the first Latino American to join the Astronaut Corps."*

I looked up everything I could about this man, even finding a photograph of him. As I learned more about Dr. Chang Díaz, I got goose bumps realizing that my story paralleled his. I also envisioned accomplishing the same things he had. In a sense, I was jealous, but it was what I thought of as a healthy type of jealousy. Dr. Chang Díaz was an immigrant who came from humble beginnings like me, who spoke English with an accent like me, and, most important, who looked like me! If someone else who had an upbringing similar to mine was able to achieve his life goal of becoming an astronaut, why couldn't I? This was when I challenged and promised myself that I would do everything within my abilities to someday be selected as a NASA astronaut.

Now I was even more optimistic about my future, or *futuro*. The following day in class, I sat in my seat, eager to learn like never before. I knew the more knowledge I consumed, the better equipped I would be for the dream job that would one day literally take me out of this world.

I excelled in all subjects, especially math and science. My grades were excellent, and college was my next stop. I began researching different engineering programs at various local universities. In doing so, I confirmed something I already suspected—that the cost of attending college was extremely high. I had no choice but to start looking for scholarships, or *becas*.

"*Señora* Bello, I don't know what to do," I said to her one day after sitting in her biology class as she was erasing the chalkboard. "I want to go to college, but..."

"But what?" she asked as she shook the chalk off her hands.

I confessed to her that I did not know how I was going to pay for college and that I needed a *beca*.

By this time, I had already decided that I wanted to study what I considered the most difficult branch of engineering: electrical engineering. This was a consideration that I shared with *señora* Bello.

"Very good, José. A lot of astronauts study either mechanical or electrical engineering in college."

"You remember me telling you that I want to be an astronaut?"

"Of course. I haven't forgotten. I know we only talked

about it twice, but I remember. Let's see what the counseling center can do to help you apply for scholarships this year."

*Señora* Bello—who was now teaching science in high school—offered to help me find a scholarship, and she even helped me fill out some of the applications. My history teacher, Mr. Salvador Zendejas, was the biggest help in finding me schools with scholarship opportunities. Years earlier, he had helped me appreciate and embrace my Mexican culture; now he was helping me research various engineering programs that would best suit me. He also helped me with my college applications and edited the essays I attached to each application, where I explained why I wanted to attend that particular school. Honestly, I do not know what I would have done without the guidance of these two great teachers, along with that of my math teacher, Mr. Dave Ellis.

After I graduated from Franklin, I maintained communication with all my favorite teachers and classmates. As for Mr. Zendejas, I never had the opportunity to formally thank him for helping me apply to college. And I must admit, I did not make a great effort in tracking him down. Years later, I learned that he died in an automobile accident. Upon learning of this, I could not forgive myself for the longest time for not taking the time to simply thank him for his guidance and help. This also taught me one of life's greatest lessons: Always make the time today to thank the people around you, because tomorrow may be too late.

After being accepted at various universities, I chose to go to the University of the Pacific, which is located in my hometown of Stockton. I made this choice for three reasons: It had a solid engineering program; it offered me a great scholarship; and I could live at home, thus allowing me to save costs on room, board, and meals. The scholarship came from the Community Involvement Program, or CIP Program, as we referred to it. This program, still in existence today, is designed to help local area students attend the University of the Pacific by providing financial aid of up to 90 percent of the tuition cost. This, coupled with the fact that I would still live at home, easily made Pacific my best option.

I remember telling my mother I was accepted to Pacific the moment I received my admittance letter: *"Mamá!* I got in! I got in! I'm going to go to college!" I yelled as I ran into the kitchen, where she was washing the dishes.

"What? I can't believe it!" she said as she dropped the plastic plate in the kitchen sink out of excitement. "Salvador! Our youngest *hijo* is going to college!"

My father came into the kitchen as soon as he heard what my mother said; this was the moment he had been looking forward to for over seventeen years. He always knew his hard work and his sacrifices would pay off one day, and now the last of his four children was accepted into a university.

"The rest is up to you now, *mi hijo*, my son. Work hard and don't let anything stand in your way. We are very proud of you." He paused to take in the moment. "You won't be a poor *campesino* worker like me now."

*"Papá!* You are not a poor peasant worker. You're more than that. You and *Mamá* are amazing people and good examples to us, your children." His eyes were instantly filled with tears. All he could do was give me a big bear hug.

"You're an example to me," he confessed.

When my four years at Franklin were coming to an end, I could not help but feel nostalgic when I realized that I would no longer serve my classmates as their student body president. This also meant that Mr. Ellis, Mr. Zendejas, and *señora* Bello would no longer be my teachers. As I was walking down the hallway, days before graduation, I stopped and realized one thing: Life is made up of different epochs, which lead to other bigger and better ones.

"What are you planning to do after you graduate?" I asked Carlos.

"Well, it doesn't look like I get to walk the line and graduate since I don't have all my credits. So, I don't know what I'll do. Maybe take the GED test, maybe get a job, or...I don't know. Maybe I'll do both? My brother told me he would help me find a job that pays a lot."

"You don't plan on continuing your education?" I asked him.

"You sound just like my mom. You already know what I think about school," he said as he rolled his eyes.

"Just don't rule it out completely. It's for your future," I advised him.

"Let's go. You're always talking about the future."

Years later and after drifting apart, I would find out that he indeed did not continue his education. He ended up doing low-skilled work in low-paying jobs. *Las drogas*, or drugs, robbed his brother Alberto of his future. They found Alberto's lifeless body in his apartment; an autopsy later revealed that he died of a drug overdose, probably as a result of heroin or cocaine use. As for my neighbor Sergio, he too did not have an opportunity to make something of himself. One day years later, as I was getting an award for one my projects at Lawrence Livermore National Laboratory, I received a call from my mother who told me that neighbors stumbled upon his body, which was hanging from a tree in the park. To my knowledge, no arrests were made in connection to his death. It remains unclear as to whether it was a suicide or a homicide.

I truly believe my friends were not the individuals they appeared to be. They were just three little boys, or *chamacos*, who needed role models in their lives to steer them in the right direction. If someone would have made them realize the importance of going to school or infused them with self-confidence, their destinies, or *destinos*, would have been very different. When I received word of their deaths, I felt impotent, wondering if perhaps I could have done something to help them make the right decisions. However, I was too young and naive to recognize the warning signs of their troubles, let alone interfere in their lives.

Today, I reminisce while looking at photographs of the four of us in our adolescent years. There is a picture of us posing in our baggy clothes, with defiant looks on our faces and our arms folded upright, leaning against my 1964 black Chevy Impala lowrider. *Las memorias*, or the memories, of the times we spent together and the laughs we shared rush back into my mind. At times, I even recall the moments when we confronted other *chamacos* who we thought were threatening our territory. Not a day goes by where I am not thankful to God for protecting my family and me from the violence that plagued our neighborhood. A simple case of being in the wrong place at the wrong time could have easily resulted in my life turning out very differently.

I wish I had the opportunity to go back in time to help Alberto, Sergio, and Carlos make the right choices.

Unfortunately, I do not. The only thing I can do for them now is honor the memory of Alberto and Sergio in this book.

On graduation day, I stood in line with the rest of my class, dressed in my olive green cap and gown. I confess, I was scared at the thought of having to venture into the real world. This meant that I had to start a new chapter in my quest to reach my lifelong dream.

My family was seated in the audience waiting for my name to be called to receive my high school diploma. When I saw my parents' faces in the audience, I no longer saw their youth and strength. Years of hard labor in the fields had stripped them of it. My siblings were no longer *joven*, or young. Leticia already had one child with her husband, Gabriel. Gil was nineteen years old, and Salvador was about to graduate from *la Universidad San Nicolás de Hidalgo* in the city of Morelia, the capital of Michoacán.

After the ceremony, I posed for pictures with my family, aunts, and uncles. Then, the hugs and kisses followed before the final good-byes to my classmates and teachers. I saw *señora* Bello approach my mother.

"José is an extraordinary young man. You did a fine job raising him," she told her.

"*Muchas gracias,*" I heard my mother say to her.

Afterward, my mother could not help but be proud. The look on her face after *señora* Bello walked away made my graduation day all the more special.

A few weeks before classes began, my family decided to take a trip to La Piedad to visit my *abuelitos*, who were not aware that I had been accepted to a university.

My mornings, afternoons, and nights during this particular trip were spent no differently from the ones of my childhood. It appeared to me that time in La Piedad had stood still, but my grandparents' gray hair reminded me that time is an unforgiving element.

Although many years had gone by, my *abuela* Chayito still kissed me good night on my forehead, just as she did when I was a child. I remember feeling her warm lips on my forehead, and I can still recall the sound her heart made when she would lean down to kiss me and whisper, *"Buenas noches, Pepito."* I remember eating *tamales* and drinking *atole* for breakfast in the mornings with my family before we would head out to enjoy the day on the veranda of the dam. This was the exact same location where I would daydream for hours sitting next to my *abuelito* José. Both of us would gaze up at the night sky and patiently wait to see a shooting star.

During one afternoon in particular, I was alone, thinking about the future. My siblings had already started making their life choices as I was just about to start my first year in college. My head was filled with countless questions, doubts, and fears; I did not know what to expect. Needless to say, I was confused. The only thing that could put my mind at ease was watching the sunset glisten in the water of the dam.

What was going on with me? Why was I suddenly beginning to have doubts? I remembered Carlos's theory about the lack of opportunity that people with brown skin had in the U.S. as a result of discrimination. I also remembered *la señora* Bello's and Ms. Young's words of encouragement, my father's advice, and my mother's expectations. I spent the next few days amid deep confusion.

\*  \*  \*

It turned out that I was not the only one with a burden. The look on my father's face told me that there was something bothering him. For many years, he had been building a house on his native soil in La Piedad. During this trip, he had hoped to finish building our *casa*, but things were not going according to plan. My father's concern was that he was building a house for the family—but his kids were all grown up and each of them was parting ways with their parents. Was it worth continuing to pursue his dream of finishing the *casita*? I overheard a conversation between my father and grandfather on this matter, and what I learned from that conversation gave me the strength to make my important life decisions at the time.

"You're not going to have enough money to finish your house on this trip, Salvador," said his father, my grandfather José.

"I know."

"At this rate, it'll take you at least a couple more years to finish it."

"But I'll finish it."

It took my father over ten years to finish building his dream house, which he had designed himself. In fact, he had designed a 3-D model of the house from cardboard before beginning its construction. In the end, the real house looked exactly like the model he had built years earlier.

I considered my father my hero as I saw the determination and confidence in his eyes that day when he told my grandfather that he would finish building his house. That same determination and confidence rubbed off on me, and it propelled me to make my own *sueño* a reality. He committed himself to building his house because he knew his faith would carry him through. The foundation for the rest of my own life had been laid then and there. Once you start something, you have to finish it.

I had to be determined and perseverant to become an astronaut. It became the philosophy I lived by from that moment on. My mother taught me the importance of having objectives in life from which others can benefit as well. My mother would have me ponder the answer to this question: *What is the purpose of being wealthy and successful if you cannot share it?*

My parents, despite their limited resources, never stopped lending a hand to others. My father helped my aunts, uncles, and cousins from Mexico file for their immigration *papeles*, or green cards, so they could legally work in the fields of the United States. It was common for other relatives to live with us for long periods of time until they were able to begin their lives anew on their own. Even during the most adverse times, my father never stopped helping others. That is why, to this day, many people remember him for being the generous and humble man that he is. It is a profound thing when someone can leave behind such a powerfully positive legacy.

CHAPTER 4

# Following My Dream

*The imprint of a dream is no less real than that of a
footstep.*

GEORGES DUBY (1919–1996)
FRENCH HISTORIAN

In July 1980, during my orientation session on the University of the Pacific campus, I ran into *señora* Bello. She was on campus attending some type of teacher recertification class. After our initial greetings and exchanging of pleasantries, she expressed her concern for how I would adjust to college life; she warned me that even though I managed to stay clear of drugs in my neighborhood, the college environment would be just as challenging. At that point, I realized she was more than just a former high school teacher: She was more like a second mother. Her words of encouragement and advice always gave me that extra confidence I needed to continue moving forward.

"You're all grown up now, José. You're about to turn eighteen and embark upon your college career. You know, I was young once and in college just like you. I know the challenges you're going to face. The only thing I ask of you is not to forget who you are and where you come from. Don't allow anything, or anyone, to deter you from your schoolwork," she told me as we walked toward the student center together to get coffee.

"Don't worry. I won't," I assured her.

"Do you still want to be an astronaut?"

"Of course I do."

"Well then, you will be. I'm sure of that. Don't ever stop dreaming, José, because to stop dreaming is to stop living."

There has never been a moment when I have ceased to dream, or *soñar*. It was one of the lessons she taught me. As I arrived home that day, I performed my usual ritual of looking up in the sky and daydreaming of what my future could hold.

My constant worry over what the next four years would bring was enough to keep me awake the entire night before my first day of college. I thought back to my first day of elementary school when I was entering a new environment; it was the same feeling all over again. It was as if the film of my childhood had rewound, except I was living it again as a young adult. I remember back then sitting quietly at my desk, staring at all the new faces around me, and being afraid to reach out to others or introduce myself. I would make it a point to be more assertive, promising myself to turn over a new page as I began a new stage of my life. Then, as I tossed and turned in my bed, I saw my new notebooks full of blank pages. The sight reminded me that I was starting from zero once again, but I knew that new opportunities were sure to present themselves. I was excited as I imagined the possibilities that these opportunities could hold. I fell asleep with those thoughts.

Although I lived just twenty minutes from campus, I woke up very early the next morning so I would not be late on my first day. I was dressed and ready to go by seven in the morning even though my first class did not begin until nine.

The first thing I did when I woke up was put my notebooks, pens, and pencils in my backpack. Then, I tried on many different shirts and pants to see which would look best on me. After numerous changes, I decided to go with a pair of Levi's jeans and an olive-green polo shirt. By this point, I had created piles of clothes on the floor. I quickly put on my white tennis shoes. I felt it was the perfect outfit because it did not attract too much attention, yet it still made me look presentable. It was clear to me that starting college meant making a transition that consisted of not only retiring my baggy pants and changing how I dressed, but also of making new friends who would come from completely different backgrounds. The one thing that did bridge my transition to college life was my 1964 Chevrolet Impala Super Sport. This was more out of necessity, since I needed my car to get to school, and I certainly could not afford what would be considered a more mainstream vehicle.

Before I sat down to eat breakfast, I looked at myself in the mirror to make sure my hair and budding mustache were perfect.

"You are so handsome," I heard my mother say as I was standing in front of the mirror.

"*Gracias, Mamá*," I replied, a bit embarrassed at being caught looking at myself.

"Breakfast is ready," she announced.

"I'll be right there."

She then approached me from behind and said, "The girls are not going to be able to control themselves when they see you. I bet you'll even find yourself a nice college girl."

"*Ay Mamá!* Please," I responded. "What girl will be

interested in someone who doesn't have a single penny to his name?"

"Well, you will once you graduate."

I did not continue the conversation.

I cannot help but laugh when I think back at how I was constantly worrying about my family's financial situation and thinking about ways to improve our plight instead of focusing on finding a *muchacha*. My father and brothers always teased me by telling me that if I did not find a girlfriend, I would end up being a priest instead of an engineer. But at the time, my main objective was to stay focused and graduate from college. Then I could worry about finding the love of my life. That was a decision, it turned out, that I never regretted.

The movies and television shows I watched growing up led me to believe that everyone in college was friendly. They also led me to believe that both class and cultural differences were not taken into account by faculty and fellow students. Unfortunately, after arriving on campus, I quickly realized that college life seemed to mimic what I had experienced all my life.

Newer-model sports cars outnumbered all the vehicles of other makes and models in the university's parking lots; my old black '64 Chevy Impala was a far cry from the luxury afforded by the shiny, new, horsepower-heavy models that surrounded it. My car was in such poor condition that every time I pulled out of my parking spot, I would see a big black spot as a result of the oil that leaked from the engine. I was clearly surrounded by students who came from families of means. I, in contrast, was on financial aid, held a part-time job, and supplemented my income with an additional work-study job on campus.

After running all over campus to get things done, I took

a break to sit down on a bench. I sensed that someone was staring at me from a distance. I looked up and noticed it was James, the same James who tormented me in elementary school by calling me names and making fun of me for bringing tacos for lunch. We made eye contact and looked at each other for a brief moment; I acknowledged his presence with the nod of my head, coupled with a courteous smile. He, in turn, did not acknowledge my presence but had a puzzled look on his face as if to say, "What are you doing here at Pacific?"

The awkwardness of the moment made me get up to go to the bathroom. As I washed my hands, I reflected and thought to myself that I no longer wanted to be scrutinized or made to feel like I had to justify myself. That was the past, and I was living in the present.

I was focusing on my future when I suddenly heard "Hey, how are you doing?" from behind me.

"Hi," I responded.

"My name is Ervin, what's yours?" he asked politely.

"José, José Hernández," I responded.

This is how I met Ervin, a Venezuelan of Romanian descent, who later became one of my best friends in college.

"Are you a freshman?" he asked.

"Yes."

"I am too! Hey, we might even have a class together."

"Maybe. I have physics right now," I told him.

"Me too! Let's go!"

From the moment I first stepped foot into the freshman physics classroom, I knew the material being taught was not going to be easy. I had a feeling deep inside my heart that math was no longer going to be good to me.

"Good morning, class. I'm Professor Andrés Rodríguez. I will be teaching you physics. Are there any questions?" Dr. Rodríguez was a very short man with silvery-white hair who always seemed to have an unlit cigar—used more like a pacifier—in his mouth or hand. He talked with a heavy accent. Because of the cigar, I guessed he was of Cuban descent. Later, I would find my assumption to be correct.

"Will a syllabus be handed out?" asked a female classmate very hesitantly.

"Syllabus? There's no need for one. The curriculum of this class is going to be something none of you have seen before. It's not going to make any sense without me personally guiding you throughout the semester. Let's begin, shall we?" I shivered with goose bumps when I heard him speak in what I thought was an unfriendly tone.

Looking around the classroom and seeing all the new faces once again brought back the same feelings I had while in elementary school, when I was trying to figure out what the writing on the chalkboard meant. The only difference now was that the board was plastered with symbols and numbers, not words in a foreign language I did not know.

Just ten minutes into his lecture, I was beginning to think there was no way I would ever pass his class. The chalkboard was filling up with one physics formula after another. I might as well have been staring at Egyptian hieroglyphics. *El profesor* Rodríguez was talking and writing so quickly that I could barely keep up. I just wrote down everything he wrote as fast as I could without understanding any of it.

"Any questions?" he asked.

No one raised a hand.

"Don't ever be left with any doubts or questions. Better to be ignorant for a moment than for life. If you don't understand something, simply ask." This was an anecdotal piece of advice I remembered Dr. Jones giving to all freshmen of the Community Involvement Program (CIP) during orientation. Dr. Jones added, "Always sit in the front rows of the classroom." This was something I also did. Dr. Jones was the director of the CIP, and his job was to see that all of the students with a CIP scholarship succeeded at Pacific. The CIP office turned out to be my primary center of support, and it was the first place I felt at home while on the Pacific campus. In the coming months and years, I would not only greatly benefit from their tutoring services, but I would also utilize their facility as a place to study before my final exams.

I took a deep breath and as I exhaled, I dared to raise my hand.

"Professor Rodríguez, I really don't understand *anything* you just wrote on the board."

Some of my classmates began to laugh, making me feel like an idiot for even raising my hand.

*El profesor* Rodríguez looked at me, smiled, and asked, "What's your name?"

"José," I responded.

"Well, José, the reason why you don't understand anything that I just wrote is because it's nonsense. It's a joke and if you all look closely, you will see that it was a lesson in disguise," he revealed.

Everyone became silent, embarrassed by both their own ignorance and their fear of not speaking up. They all seemed to wish that they had found themselves asking for clarification when they did not understand the professor's scribbles on the board, either.

When my last class ended, I recounted my day as I walked to my car to go home.

Awkward Moments: 2

Friends: 1

Life Lessons: 1

Fulfilled Expectations: 50%, for now

Overall, a good day, I thought. I looked up at the sky and saw the moon looking down at me, just like it did when I was little and on my way to La Piedad. There was never a time that it lost sight of me, which, as a child, made me feel special.

I took physics, chemistry, calculus, and FORTRAN computer programming during my first semester at Pacific. All four were equally difficult and required many hours of studying.

By this time, however, I was eighteen, and I could work in the canneries. During the summer, my high school counselor, Mr. Vance Paulson, worked in the personnel department of a particular cannery located a few blocks from my home. He always made an effort to get summer jobs for his high school graduate students at the cannery, especially those with good grades. The only issue was that the cannery season ran into the beginning of my college school year and made my transition into college even more difficult. Nevertheless, for the first month or two of college, I would work the 10 p.m. to 6 a.m. graveyard shift, go home, bathe, and then head to class.

After the cannery season, I would return to my regular job as a busboy at a local Mexican restaurant. This was a job I was not too fond of, as I worked evenings and weekends while enrolled in the academically challenging Pacific engineering program. Often I also had to deal with customers who believed they had the right to mistreat employees with brown skin. I lost count of the times I wanted to quit, an action I did not go through with after I learned to ignore the behavior of rude patrons. After each shift, I went home to do my homework and study. My daily routine kept me busy; I seldom had free time. The uncertainty of my financial situation, along with the difficulty of the classes I was enrolled in, soon began to overwhelm me.

"But math is supposed to be my best friend," I told myself, looking at my physics notes. It got to the point where I no longer thought I was going to be able to handle it. My mind and body were tired of staying up late at night as I was trying to do my homework. I saw Dr. Rodríguez walking toward me just then.

"What's wrong, José?"

"Nothing."

"Are you sure?" he asked as he looked down at my notes for his class. "The look on your face tells me otherwise. I think I know what's wrong."

"You do?" I asked.

"Sooner or later, something will come along that challenges you to the point where you don't think you'll be able to handle it. But this is not one of those things. You are intelligent, José. You just have to keep at it until you master it, which you will. I promise." He put his hand on my shoulder as if he was giving me some fatherly advice.

"You're right, Professor Rodríguez. I'm having trouble in your class, and I think I am going to find someone to tutor me."

"Sounds like a great plan. You just need some extra time to grasp the concepts. I think you have what it takes to be an excellent engineer. The only thing that worries me is your temptation to give up. I've seen you be a bit quieter than normal; you don't smile as much anymore. Anything else going on, José?"

"It's everything. I feel like an outsider at this university. Maybe it's because I don't live on campus or drive a shiny new car. Perhaps my skin color has something to do with it. I don't understand what I'm being taught, and I don't have time to study because I have to work to be able to pay for school. Maybe I'm just looking for excuses. I don't know. Perhaps I'm not cut out for college."

"José, don't you ever say that again! Of course you're cut out for college. Don't feel like an outsider. If you do, then always invite yourself back in! You know you had to meet the same entrance requirements as any of the other students, and no one has done anything special for you to be here. You've earned it, so you need to start behaving like you belong because you do! You will always encounter bigotry and hate everywhere you go. What makes a person great is how he handles that type of adversity. The most important thing is not what others see when they look at you, but what you see when you look inside of yourself. You are going to be a great engineer one day. If that is not enough, think of why you want to be an engineer, and use that to fuel your drive. I am sure your parents are proud of you now that you are here at Pacific."

Dr. Rodríguez had hit me with a one-two punch. He made

me realize that, first and foremost, I needed to continue for my parents' sake. All the sacrifices they had made for me should not be for naught. Imagining the look on my mother's face if I had to tell her I was dropping out of college was enough to make me regroup and try even harder. Second, my childhood dream was to be an *astronauta*, and that was not going to happen until I was an engineer. I quickly convinced myself both to continue working even harder and to use the resources at CIP, which included tutoring assistance. I got as much help as I could, all in an effort to avoid becoming a dropout statistic.

The word *dream*, which at one point in my childhood was my favorite word, was no longer in my vocabulary. It was time to start making dreams a reality. To stop working toward making my dreams come true is to stop living, I thought, as *el profesor* Rodríguez walked away.

I got up and started to walk to the library in a pensive state of mind when I accidently bumped into a fellow student.

"I'm so sorry," I said to him, as I helped him pick up his books from the ground.

"It's okay," he said.

"Are you heading to the library?" he asked in Arabic.

"What?" I said.

"Are you heading to the library?" he said again in Arabic.

"I'm sorry, I don't understand you. I don't speak Arabic," I replied.

"I'm sorry; you look like a Saudi. Are you heading to the library?" he repeated in English this time.

"Yes. I have to check out a few chemistry reference books," I said to him before I introduced myself. "My name is José."

"Hello. My name is Amin. I too am heading to the library to return these books."

We shook hands and then walked together to the library, or *la biblioteca*.

Amin soon became another one of my best friends. I did not know too much about him at first because he never talked about his life; however, judging by the late-model Porsche he drove, he was certainly a person of means. There were times when I wanted to pry into his life, but I did not. It was not until much later, when reading *Forbes* magazine, that I discovered that his family was one of the wealthiest in the Middle East. The article went on to describe the holdings that made up their vast wealth. I could not believe my eyes. However, this new piece of information did not affect our friendship at all. He remains one of my best friends to this day, and he is a very humble man, especially given his economic status.

"Engineering is really hard, don't you think?" asked Amin as we both looked for our books in the science section of the library.

"I agree."

"I saw you talking with Professor Rodríguez earlier. Are you having trouble in his class? I can tutor you, if you want."

"Oh, no. I'm not. Thank you anyway."

"Very well. If you ever need anything, or someone to study with, just let me know. The last thing we both need is to fail his class."

"I will. Thanks."

I continued searching for my books, but from the corner of my eye, I could see that he was still looking at me. He seemed unconvinced by my assertion that I did not need help.

"I found my book, José. It was nice meeting you. I'll see you in class tomorrow."

"See you tomorrow."

Later I thought about his offer, and it made me realize that no one can succeed in life without the help or support of others. It was as if the universe was purposely putting people in my path to help me continue forward, despite my current state of mind. It was no different at home.

When I arrived home that day, my mother was talking on the phone with my *tía* Rosa, one of my father's sisters from La Piedad.

"*Sí*, Rosa. Who would have thought? My Pepito is going to be an engineer. He got a scholarship too. He's always been so smart. I cannot wait until he graduates. I'm not going to be able to hold back tears when he does."

That moment was my epiphany. I had recently failed to remember my dream. I studied simply to study, and I worked simply to work, without remembering the reason why I was doing what I was doing. My mother believed in what I was doing. Though she acknowledged how hard I studied and worked, she spoke with such confidence in discussing what the future had in store for me and the rest of the family. The smile on her face as she conversed with my *tía* Rosa reinforced that I could not give up, not now, not ever.

"*Hijo*, you're home. Are you hungry?" she asked.

"*Sí, Mamá*," I said, as if pretending I did not hear her conversation with *tía* Rosa.

Pacific boasted a diverse group of students from a multitude of ethnic and financial backgrounds. Luckily, my friends and I did not pay attention to any racial, language, or financial differences that existed between us. After settling in at Pacific, finding and making friends turned out to be easier than I expected, despite obvious cultural, social, and economic differences.

The third person who became a great friend to me at Pacific was Don. He was Vietnamese and was also from Stockton. He spent the majority of his time studying. His father was on the school of engineering faculty at Pacific. Don was a straight-A student, but he perpetually worried about his academic performance. He knew that his father could easily speak with any of his teachers to find out how he was doing in their classes.

"Are you guys going to the fraternity party tonight?" asked Ervin, as we were sitting on a bench just outside the engineering building.

"No. I have to study," Don answered quickly to keep Ervin from convincing him to go. "We have a test on Monday; we better study instead."

"You're so boring, Don. José? Amin? What do you guys say? You guys going? I'm going because a good-looking girl invited me," informed Ervin.

Ervin spent most of his time talking about his multiple conquests and how he was able to win over girls. He also bragged about the many broken hearts he left along the way.

We did accompany him to some of the frat parties on campus. I must admit that the parties proved to be a bit overwhelming for me at times. That is not to say that I did not enjoy spending time there, but I am sure many of the other attendees did not have to work and go to school at the same time. For them, a late night of partying was usually followed by sleeping in the following day. I did not have that luxury as I either had to catch up on my studying or go to work. Most of my friends had their future pretty much secured after graduation: Amin had a position waiting for him at his father's company; IBM had offered Don an entry-level position; Ervin had plans to return to Venezuela to take over the family business. I, on the other hand, had nothing to look forward to—at least not yet.

"What do you plan to do after you graduate, José?" Every time I was asked this question, I did not know how to answer. Should I have answered, "Become an astronaut"? Instead, I answered differently every time. One time I even answered, "I'm probably going to go into politics."

"Why politics?" they asked.

"Because there has to be a way to combine politics and engineering that would allow me to help a lot of people."

"So you don't want to be an engineer anymore?" asked Amin. I did not answer him.

"Hey, everyone! José is going to be a politician," Ervin said with a bit of sarcasm.

"I think José will make a great politician. Hey, he might even go on to become governor!" said Don in my defense.

From that moment on, they started to refer to me as "the *gober*." *Gober* means "to govern," and this seemed appropriate since they thought I could one day be the governor, or *gobernador*. I always thought *Gober* was a far better nickname than the one they would have given me had I told them the truth about wanting to become an astronaut.

My *futuro*, or future, was still uncertain as of December 1980. There were not enough hours in the day for me to go to school, go to work, and study. Sleeping was something I was not getting enough of, and I could not wait for my winter break so I could finally rest. Strangely enough, when it came, I was not very excited.

On the last day of the fall semester, during my last final, I did something that I had never done before. I was the first to turn in my exam and walk out of the classroom, marking the beginning of my winter break. I was not my usual self, and I did not know why.

Later that day, my friends tried to convince me to go to the movies with them to watch *Superman II*, which was what everyone was talking about at the time. Amin wanted to spend some time together before he had to fly back to Saudi Arabia for winter break. "Come on, José, come with us to the movies!"

"I don't know."

"You barely hang out with us anymore."

"I know. I've been so busy."

"You're always busy. Just come. You have all of winter break to relax. What do you say?"

"Fine. I'll meet you guys there later."

I could not help but feel fatigued when I entered the dark theater. My lack of sleep had caused me to act differently, which everyone noticed.

As the movie progressed, my enthusiasm grew. I could not tell if it was the music or images of space or perhaps the simple distraction of hanging out with my friends, but I felt alive again—full of vigor and energy. I knew I would never be able to fly around space like Superman, but I believed that I would one day be able to float around in a zero-G environment and do my best impersonation of him.

As soon as I got home, I did something that I had not done in many months: I gazed up at the stars from my bedroom window. I thought about my past, my future, and how I would somehow achieve my dream. I stopped when I could not keep my eyes open any longer, slowly closing them in the hopes of getting a good night's rest.

Much to my dismay, I found it difficult to fall asleep. I was facedown, hugging my pillow, looking off in the direction of my slightly opened closet, and that is how I saw it. In the corner, covered with dust, was my brother's *Star Trek* model spaceship. I got up on impulse, walked over to it, and picked it up. This moment was exactly what I needed as it allowed me to reflect and take the initiative to make some changes. I decided to quit my part-time job at the restaurant, and I asked for more hours at my work-study job on campus. I reminded myself that the more time I spent on campus, the greater the opportunities I had to study and thus improve my performance.

The next afternoon as I was cleaning the model spaceship, I got the feeling that everything was going to work itself out over time. Afterward, I placed the spaceship on the shelf over my dresser so it would always serve as a visible reminder that everything was going to be just fine.

That night, I slept for more than eight hours for the first time in a long time.

Upon returning from winter break, I once again ran into the woman who had become a second mother to me over the years. I was walking toward the science laboratories—where I worked as a lab assistant—when I heard someone yell out my name.

"José, *hijo!*"

I quickly turned around and saw *señora* Bello. "*Señora* Bello!" I said in disbelief.

"How have you been?"

"Very well. Thanks."

"I can see that. You look so happy and healthy," she said, as she pinched my cheek with her maternal hand.

In addition to her regular job of teaching high school students, *la señora* Bello now taught an evening class at Pacific. Every now and then, I would see her on campus surrounded by students vying for her attention for help on their *tarea*, or homework. I felt special because she always made time to speak to me no matter how busy she was.

"I'm glad I ran into you. I wanted to speak with you about something," I said to Mrs. Bello.

"Of course. What is it?"

"I have been doubting myself lately. I did not believe I was capable of anything until I remembered that you told me I could achieve anything in life as long as I fought for it, right?"

"That's right! José, tell me the truth, do you still want to be an astronaut?" she asked in a low voice, as if wanting to keep it a golden secret.

"*Sí*, now more than ever."

"And my heart tells me that one day you will be," she confessed.

As my college career progressed, I found out more about the details of Pacific's Engineering Co-op education program. At the time, all U.S. citizens in Pacific's engineering program were required to intern with a company that allowed them to acquire experience in their field of concentration. Thus, during my junior year at Pacific, I interned at Lawrence Livermore National Laboratory, almost by accident.

I found out through pure coincidence that a representative from the Lawrence Livermore National Laboratory would be interviewing students on campus for two six-month internship positions. There were a dozen of my fellow engineering students who had already signed up, hoping to fill one of the two positions. I noticed that the last slot on the sign-up roster was open, so I quickly added my name to the list.

Later that week, dressed in the only suit and tie that I owned, I showed up at the co-op office and waited for my turn to interview. Mr. Frank Inami, a Japanese American man, finally called me in for an interview. By the end of the interview, I was certain I had made a good impression.

Too bad it seemed not to matter: "José, I would have loved to have offered you the position, but it looks like I found two students who seem to be excellent matches to the needs of our engineering department."

"That's okay, Mr. Inami. Perhaps next time; thank you for your time," I responded, trying to hide my disappointment.

Then Mr. Inami said, "José, would you be interested if I told you there was a special program set up at the laboratory through which you could possibly work for us?"

"Yes, I would! But wait, does it still pay?" I asked somewhat suspicious.

He let out a gentle laugh and said, "Yes, it pays the same amount that your fellow students will be earning. However, this program is funded out of our Office of Equal Opportunity for the sole purpose of opening doors for minority students such as yourself. So, what do you say? Are you interested?"

"Yes!" was my immediate reply.

I did not have to think twice before answering. I was happy to know that there was help for minorities and that I had found it. This was not only a job; it was an opportunity. Lawrence Livermore National Laboratory is a premier research facility dedicated to national defense and is funded through the Department of Energy. It was located just forty miles from my home, allowing me to commute to work—while I was making some money, too! I could not stop thinking of how I would feel on the first day when I would walk through those doors.

I received a call from Mr. Inami two weeks after my interview. He called to confirm my position as an engineering assistant at the laboratory. I was so grateful that I promised myself that I was going to work tirelessly to prove my worth. I did this in the hope that they would hire me the following year through traditional means for my second six-month internship and eventually for a career position. Luckily, my supervisor and coworkers were so satisfied with my performance and work ethic that they told me they would work hard to get me back for my second co-op assignment. Even better, they saw no reason why I could not get hired as a career employee once I graduated from Pacific. And that was how I came one step closer to realizing my dream.

# CHAPTER 5

# For My Mother

*If you don't know where you are going, any road will
get you there.*

I had never told my mother that she was my main motivation
for everything, which was why I thanked her on my graduation day in my own special way.

In May 1985, at the age of twenty-two, I found myself
dressed in a black-and-orange graduation gown with a
standard-issue black cap, ready for my college graduation. My
siblings—all of whom had already graduated from college—
were there along with my parents to witness my accomplishment. According to my parents, who could not stop taking
pictures of me, I looked incredible. They were so proud that
their youngest son was about to be a university graduate.

I heard my father whisper to my mother, "We raised him
right." Then I heard my mother reply, "Our sacrifices were
well worth it." They must have thought I was too wrapped up
in my own moment to hear them. Thus, I turned around and
said, "You did, *Papá*. You and *Mamá* could not have done a
better job. You're the best parents in the whole world!" The
three of us then embraced for what seemed like forever.

"It's time to go!" interrupted Lety.

The commencement speech was not only directed at the

graduates, but to everyone in attendance: *"Life will throw obstacles in your path that will prevent you from achieving your goals. Be assured that you have the power to overcome them. All of you here today have a great responsibility: you must realize your dreams—in part for those who believe in you, for the greater good of society, and most importantly, for yourself."*

One by one, *los graduados*, or the graduates, crossed the stage to receive their diplomas and shake hands, one last time, with faculty from the University of the Pacific.

When "José Hernández Moreno, cum laude" was announced, it was received with loud applause from the audience. I could hear my mother's applause as I walked across the stage to receive my diploma, because it was the loudest. With my degree in hand, I stopped to show her what I had written on top of my cap before exiting the stage. It read "Hi Mom!" or *"¡Hola Mamá!"* It was a symbol of my gratitude for everything she had done for me my entire life. I remember clearly how everyone turned to look at her as she rose from her seat, and how her crystalline eyes, which were holding back tears, met mine as she blew me a kiss.

As soon as I got off the stage, I received more congratulatory hugs and kisses before posing for more pictures. The day ended with a party that my family put together at our house. The pictures that were taken that day serve as proof of how happy and relieved I looked after years and years of hard work had come to an end.

I wasted no time in starting my career at the Lawrence Livermore National Laboratory in Livermore, California, located some forty miles west of Stockton. By now, the commute to

The plaza of La Piedad, Michoacán, where José's parents met.

José's father, Salvador, in the plaza of La Piedad, Michoacán, with his 1957 Ford Fairlane 500. Taken in 1961.

Eleven-month-old José with his then twenty-two-year-old mother, Julia. Taken in 1963.

José's mother at nineteen years old.

José's first and second grade class with teacher Ms. Young. José is in the top row, second from the right.  Ms. Young is in the bottom row, third from the right.

Christmas in Stockton, CA. José is nine years old.

José with brother Gil (right) and sister Leticia (center) after a hard day's work of hoeing at the Evo Del Carlo tomato fields near Tracy, CA.

José with his brothers after picking tomatoes. Left to right: Gil, paternal grandfather José, oldest brother Salvador, and Jose, eight years old.

José and his siblings. From top right clockwise: Gil, Salvador Jr., and Leticia. The picture was taken as a Mother's Day gift.

José's graduation photo from Franklin Senior High School in Stockton, CA, 1980.

José paying tribute to his mother, Julia, at the University of the Pacific School of Engineering graduation, with his "Hi Mom" message pasted on top of his graduation cap.

José with oldest brother Salvador Jr. at the 1985 University of the Pacific School of Engineering graduation.

Finishing his first of eleven (and counting) marathons in the Avenue of the Giants marathon in Northern California at the Humboldt Redwoods State Park.

José's inspiration, Dr. Franklin Chang Díaz, the first Latino American astronaut chosen by NASA. He was chosen during José's high school senior year. It was then that Jose promised himself to do everything possible to get selected as a NASA astronaut.

T-38 jets used for astronaut crew resource training.

José's first official portrait as a U.S. astronaut.

The nineteenth class of astronauts consisted of eleven U.S. and three Japanese astronauts. The fourteen-member class was chosen in 2004.

José and the rest of the nineteenth class of astronauts visiting the Orbiter Processing Facilities as part of their astronaut candidate training curriculum. The shuttle Atlantis is in the background getting processed for an upcoming launch.

Simulated helicopter water
rescue exercises at the Neutral
Buoyancy Laboratory.

José participating
in water survival
training at the
Neutral Buoyancy
Lab pool.

Water survival
training at the
Neutral Buoyancy
Laboratory.

At the 2006 University of the Pacific commencement with actor/director Clint Eastwood and famous jazz musician and University of the Pacific alum Dave Brubeck. José was the University's commencement speaker and both Clint Eastwood and José were awarded an honorary doctorate degree.

Getting ready for a T-38 flight from Ellington Field in Houston to the Kennedy Space Center in Florida.

U.S.A.F. SERIAL NO 63-8200

Official STS-12 mission poster. "Racking Up Science" was the official theme for this mission.

the lab was all too familiar to me since I had worked both of my co-op job assignments there. My boss, Mike Ong, made sure a career offer had come to me early in my senior year. He did this—he once told me—on purpose so that I would relax and not go through the trouble of applying to other locations, thus preventing me from being tempted by other offers. His plan proved to be mostly successful, even when I somehow managed to get an on-site interview with AT&T followed by a subsequent job-site interview. The problem was that AT&T's job was in Columbus, Ohio, which I considered to be too far from California.

As I started work at the lab, the first couple of days came and went without incident until one day when I answered a telephone call in my new office.

"Hello," I answered.

"Hello. I'm trying to reach a janitor," said the caller on the other end of the line.

"I'm afraid you have the wrong number."

"Oh. I'm sorry."

"It's okay. Have a good day," I said before I hung up.

Over the next few hours, I kept on receiving similar calls from different people at the laboratory asking for a janitor.

*"Am I speaking to the janitor?"*

*"One of the bathrooms needs soap and toilet paper."*

*"I need someone to clean my office."*

*"I need my trash emptied."*

I told each and every caller the same thing every time: "I am not the janitor; you have the wrong number."

The more phone calls I received, the more I began to realize that it was not simply a case of everyone dialing the wrong number. By that time, I had run out of patience. The only way I could make certain that the phone calls stopped was to speak to the building operator who was in charge of transferring them.

"Excuse me, Miss. I'm José Hernández, the new engineer," I said to the young woman at the front desk.

*"Engineer?"* she said in disbelief with one arched eyebrow.

"Yes. I keep getting these strange calls requesting janitorial support."

"Mr. Hernández, I'm so sorry. We had several new employees start working in this building this week. I must be sending the calls to the wrong number!" She smiled and again apologized, halfheartedly. "I'm sorry. It's just that they didn't tell us who was who."

Later that day, I found out that two of us did indeed start working in that building during the same week: José Hernández, the newly graduated engineer, and Brian Johnson, the newly hired custodian.

I would be lying to say that I was not offended; nevertheless, I decided not to speak my mind. Instead, I chose to focus on my new job and work so hard that people would recognize me for my work. In other words, I wanted to be known as José Hernández, a talented engineer who happens to be Latino, not José Hernández, the Latino engineer who has talent. A subtle difference, perhaps, but an important one for me nonetheless.

The next few days flew by quickly, then the weeks, one after the other. Challenges came from different directions. I knew that I would ultimately compete with my colleagues for better assignments and promotions. I noticed that this prestigious research facility for the U.S. Department of Energy boasted an array of engineers and scientists, most of whom held advanced degrees. I thought about this, and I came to the conclusion that for me to flourish and successfully compete in this environment, I also needed to obtain a postgraduate degree. This realization, coupled with the fact that I could not stop thinking about how I could get into the NASA astronaut program, led me to my next big decision in life: to attend graduate school. After all, Dr. Franklin Chang Díaz had a doctorate degree, and NASA chose him to go into space.

During the early part of that summer, I was notified that I was accepted to two of the three graduate schools to which I had applied. Both the University of California at Santa Barbara and Cornell University had accepted me while, ironically, Stanford had turned me down. I say "ironically" because I already had earned twelve graduate units with Stanford through their Televised Graduate Program during my two co-op stints at the lab. I spoke to my boss, Mike Ong, about my desire to pursue graduate school. I told him of my plan to spend as little time away from the Lab as possible and asked for a one-year leave of absence. I needed only a year because of my previous graduate school course work. Furthermore, I explained to him that I had already been accepted to two schools and was leaning toward the master's degree program in electrical engineering, with an emphasis in signal and systems, at the University of California at Santa Barbara.

What Mike Ong told me next somewhat concerned me. He advised me not to take a leave of absence but rather to resign from the lab. He informed me that if I remained on the payroll I would receive only a symbolic raise upon my return with a master's degree. However, if I resigned altogether, then the lab would be forced to compete with private industry for my services and I could negotiate a better salary. He assured me that he would make every effort to rehire me after I completed my degree. Truth be told, I felt resigning had some risks, as a hiring freeze could easily be implemented during my hiatus. Worse yet, he could be trying to get rid of me! Eventually I convinced myself that, in the event of a hiring freeze, I could land another job somewhere in Silicon Valley. In the event that he was trying to get rid of me, then I was fine with that too since I did not want to be in a place where I was not wanted. Luckily, though, Mike Ong was true to his word. Twelve months later, I was offered a job in his same work group at a substantially higher salary.

Graduate school was a significantly different experience for me, compared to undergraduate school. Thanks in part to my savings and a full-ride scholarship from the Graduate Engineering Minority (GEM) program, I was able to enroll in the master's program at the University of California at Santa Barbara. For the first time in my life, I did not worry about dividing my time between work and school. I even had time for my family! Having the funds to pay for college made such a difference. Now I had time to get my schoolwork done and socialize, unlike in my undergraduate days when I was working multiple jobs and going without much sleep.

It was exciting to be able to live on my own with two friends who were also Pacific alumni. One was in the graduate mechanical engineering program, and the other was working on a doctorate degree in psychology. We had parties and stayed up into the early morning hours a number of times, but we never allowed that to interfere with our studies.

Graduate school was a fast-paced program, but it did not matter. School was my full-time job, so I could spend as much time as I needed concentrating on fulfilling my responsibilities. Having left home for the first time and being able to successfully balance a demanding graduate program also gave me a sense of pride and accomplishment. I felt myself reaching a new level of maturity. The year passed quickly, and soon I found myself with another degree in hand. Finishing graduate school was yet another small step toward achieving my big dream.

With my second job offer from the lab in one hand and a master's degree in the other, I returned home to Stockton, California. After years of living in financial uncertainty, I was now about to earn—in my opinion—a decent income. The American Dream was now mine for the taking.

After I returned from Santa Barbara, I continued to live with and help out my parents. During that year, I was able to not only save a significant part of my income, but I was also able to buy myself—for the very first time—a new car. I remember it vividly; it was a 1987 gold-colored Mazda RX-7. It was a far cry from my 1964 Chevy Impala Super Sport. I liked the RX-7 because it looked so much like a Porsche.

Upon saving enough money for a down payment, I decided to invest in a new *casa* in one of the nicest neighborhoods in Stockton. I bought a modest-sized house because I still wanted the financial freedom of being able to help my parents. The neighboring homes—with green, manicured lawns and trimmed trees—that surrounded my house were picture-perfect. I looked forward to venturing out on my own but also knew that it was going to take some time for me to get accustomed to living by myself. The thought of being able to host *carne asadas,* or barbecues, for my friends and family was truly exciting. Everything was falling into place—it appeared that life was perfect. However, not even a month after moving in, everything changed one morning when I received a disturbing call from a friend. Upon hearing what he had to say, I hung up and quickly went outside to pick up the paper. The morning newspaper confirmed the news I heard over the phone: "COUPLE MURDERED IN STOCKTON: Burglar Stabs Couple to Death After Being Confronted."

I was not one to read the newspaper so early in the morning, but I desperately wanted to find out more details about the tragic news I had just heard. The article confirmed that the victims were family members from my father's side. Dumbfounded, I immediately called my parents to inform them of the tragedy, but they already knew. They were distraught, understandably so.

"We were just about to call you!" said my mother, crying over the phone.

"I'm coming over right now, *Mamá!*" I said in earnest.

I drove to my parents' house without wasting a single minute. As I neared their home, I could not help but compare their neighborhood to mine. It was as if I was comparing two completely different worlds. The situation at hand was one that I never thought we would have to deal with. I started thinking: *My parents live in a neighborhood similar to the one where my tío and tía were just murdered. How could I allow my own parents to continue living in such a place? What if what happened to my distant aunt and uncle happens to my parents?* I was not in a position to protect them because I no longer lived at home. My parents' safety was at stake here; I would not forgive myself if something ever happened to them.

As soon as I arrived at my parents' home, they were quick to tell me exactly what had happened.

"Someone broke into your aunt and uncle's house thinking no one was home. But when the intruder was confronted by your uncle and aunt, the thief killed both of them." My mother could not stop looking off into space. "Why did this happen?" she asked repeatedly.

*¿Por qué?¿Por qué?¿Por qué?*

I wish I could have answered her.

Once the mourning period was over, I still had a lot of thoughts loitering around in my head. The most burdensome of them all concerned the immediate future of my parents. I decided that the best thing for everyone would be if they moved out of the *barrio* that their children had grown up in and moved in with me. The only thing left for me to do was to convince them. I thought it would be best to bring it up to them by complaining about how difficult it was for me to maintain my house and work at the same time. The key, I thought, was to make them feel needed.

"*Mamá*, I'm constantly working and I don't have any time to clean my house, do my laundry, or even cut the grass. What should I do?"

"Well, get someone to help you with your housework one or two days a week," she said hastily.

"I wouldn't feel comfortable paying a stranger to come into my house. Maybe I should sell the house and move into an apartment."

She did not respond.

"What would you say if...well, never mind..."

"What? Tell me. You want me to come over and help you?"

"No. I was just thinking that you and *Papá* should come live with me."

"*Ay mijo*, no. What makes you think that? What would we do over there?"

"Well, you two will be there with me. What do you say, huh?"

"I don't think so. Your *papá* is not going to like the idea."

After weeks of pleading with them to move in, they finally agreed! At first, according to my mother, they felt out of place because there was not a single person in my neighborhood with whom they could speak Spanish. Also, my house was too big for her liking. As for my father—who had made a living as a truck driver transporting tomatoes from the fields to the canneries throughout California—he did not like that there was no room on my street to park his truck. In fact, the community association did not allow commercial vehicles to be parked in the neighborhood.

After a few months of living with me, my father finally confessed how he felt. "*Mijo*, I'm really not happy here," he said as we were eating dinner.

"Why?" I inquired. "It's more secure and peaceful here. Plus, we are all together."

"True. But I hate that I don't have anything to do all day. I don't like sitting around the house with nothing to do."

"There's no need for you to do anything. Everything you want, or need, I can provide," I said to him. "You don't even need to work anymore."

"I don't care! I'm not happy here! I want to work! I want to use my hands! I'm still strong!"

"Well, I'll have to find something for you to do around the house," I said.

I'm not going to deny that I was disappointed that my parents did not like living with me. The combination of hard work and sacrifice it took for me to get to where I was at that point in my life was not unlike each of the nails that were hammered into place to keep together the walls and roof of my house; the house was symbolic of my journey and a sure sign that I was on track to achieve the American Dream. However, I could not continue seeing my parents nostalgic and unhappy, because their well-being and health were important to me. I had to find a solution. Miraculously, my father came home one day with the *solución* I was looking for.

As soon as my father walked through the front door, he started shouting, *"Hijo! Hijo! Pepe!"*

"What? What's wrong?" I asked while running to see what the reason was for all the commotion.

"I was just in Lodi with my friend Jorge. We saw this nice three-acre property that's for sale. It has enough room for me to park my truck and it's nearby."

"Really? You'll have to take me to go see it right now then."

My father's mood quickly went from excited to somber.

"What's wrong?"

"I don't think I'll be able to afford it."

"And since when has money been an issue for us lately? Don't worry. We can buy it together, and it can be a good investment for us." The seriousness of his face melted away into a luminous smile.

My father and I ended up buying the property, which was actually closer to the town of Lodi, just a few minutes north of

Stockton. We all moved into the newly refurbished ranchette-style house that was situated on the lot. Even my perennial bachelor brother, Gil, decided to move in. The peace and harmony that existed there reminded me of times from my childhood that I spent in La Piedad and Ticuítaco. My parents, my brother Gil, and I wasted no time making ourselves at home on the new property, planting numerous fruit trees, plants, and a vegetable garden. It is amazing what three acres can do for a man who yearns to work with the land. To this day, now as a retired couple, my parents continue to live there. I am still convinced that the chores associated with this parcel of land are what keep them vibrant.

## "I don't think I've ever seen such beautiful eyes before!"

In the summer of 1990, my sister, Lety, and her family were shopping in the perfume section of Macy's department store in Stockton. One of the *trabajadoras*, or female employees, behind the counter caught my sister's attention, not only because she was genuinely beautiful, but also because she displayed sincere character. Adela, which I later learned was her name, had no idea that my sister was listening to a conversation she was having with a coworker. I was not there, but my sister told me what happened that day.

"Why don't you want to help those customers?" Adela inquired.

"Because I don't want to! You help them! I'm tired of dealing with them. If they live in the United States, then they should know how to speak English; I shouldn't have to speak to them in Spanish," answered Adela's frustrated coworker.

"But why? You know how to speak Spanish. It's not going to kill you. They're our customers, and they all deserve to be treated the same—regardless of what language they speak," said Adela, before she turned to the Latino customers her coworker refused to help.

"*Hola!* I'll be more than happy to help you. Tell me, what can I do for you today?"

My sister, Lety, could not stop admiring Adela from afar. She saw something special in her, which made her turn to her husband, Gabriel, and say, "I hope Pepe finds someone like her."

Later that day, Lety came over to our parents' house with groceries. It was tradition for her and my mother to cook together on the weekends. While both of them started preparing *la cena*, or dinner, I was in the living room watching television. Lety did not know I could hear her telling my mother what she had witnessed at the perfume counter earlier that day, but I heard everything she said.

"You should have seen her, *Mamá*. She had these beautiful green eyes. The way she spoke to her coworker and the way she helped her customer shows that she is a very humble and respectful young woman." I could still hear Lety, even when she lowered her voice and said to my mom, "I think she would be perfect for Pepe."

Wanting to know more about this young woman my sister could not stop talking about, I immediately got up from the couch and walked into the kitchen.

"Who is this girl you're talking about, Lety?" I asked while standing in the door frame.

"Pepe! I didn't think you could hear me," she said as she chuckled.

"What's her name?"

"I don't know. I was just telling *Mamá* she seems like a very nice girl. And since you've never had a girlfriend, perhaps you and her could, you know...," she said in an insinuating manner.

"I've had a girlfriend before!"

"Pepe, you've never had a girlfriend. Going out on a date and being in a relationship are two different things," interjected my mother, as she chopped the onions for the *pozole*, a traditional Mexican stew.

"I guess you're right. But I'll soon find the girl of my dreams. Besides, I am in no hurry! How long before dinner is ready?"

"It'll be ready soon," said my mother.

My mother was right. I'd never had a *novia*, a girlfriend. I did go out on a few dates with girls in college, none of which blossomed into serious relationships. My sister had taken it upon herself to spark my interest in a girl she thought was right for me, and—to tell the truth—she succeeded.

I went to lie on my bed until dinner was ready. Lying there, staring into space, I started imaging what the girl my sister was talking about really looked like. For all I knew, Lety was exaggerating her appearance to pique my interest. I wanted to know the color of her hair and her skin. I thought I should go to the perfume counter to see her with my own eyes.

Not a day went by when I did not think about her. I finally

gathered the courage to go to the department store where she worked. The only two things I knew about her was that she was *Mexicana* and that she had bright green *ojos*, or eyes. I quickly recognized her when I saw her behind the counter.

I peered at her almond-shaped eyes, curly black hair, and beautiful skin as I walked toward her. Lety definitely did not exaggerate how beautiful she was. She was busy with a customer when I approached the counter; I did not dare bother her. I was content just to look at her...

"Lety! I saw her!"

"So, what did you think?"

"*Está bonita,*" I said, letting my sister know how pretty I thought Adela was.

"*Bonita?* I think someone's in love," she said excitedly. "What did you say to her?"

"Nothing. I just looked at her."

"What? *Pepe!* Why didn't you talk to her?"

I do not know why she even asked; she knew I was shy.

"I'll talk to her for you," Lety said.

"Really?" I asked with a big smile.

"Yes."

"Thanks. I hope she does not already have a boyfriend," I said. I hugged my sister while she was laughing.

The next day Lety went to the department store to speak to her on my behalf. That was when Lety found out that the mystery woman's name was Adela and that she was from Cotija, Michoacán. Cotija is roughly a two-hour drive from my parents' hometown of La Piedad. A good omen, I thought! My sister also learned that Adela had just ended a relationship with her boyfriend and that she was brokenhearted. Lety continued to sporadically visit Macy's perfume department over the course of the next couple of months to build a rapport with Adela. It proved successful because, after about six months, she finally convinced Adela to go out on a blind date with me. Years later, Adela confessed to me that the only reason she agreed to go on the date with me was to stop my sister from pestering her about getting to know me.

I made sure that I arrived on time for my first date with Adela. The plan was to meet her at the end of her shift and take her to dinner. My heart was beating a bit faster than normal, my hands were sweating, and my lips were quivering; in short, I was as nervous as a teenage boy on his first date. Looking back now, I cannot help but laugh at how ridiculous I must have appeared upon our first encounter.

"Good afternoon, miss."

"Good afternoon, sir. What can I help you with today?"

"I'm looking for a young lady by the name of Adela."

"You're looking right at her."

"I'm José Hernández, Leticia's younger brother. I believe I have a date with you tonight," I said, as I wiped my sweaty palms on my jeans.

"Ah! So you're José," she responded with a smile across her face. "I get off in ten minutes. Do you mind waiting?"

"Not at all. Take your time."

We went to the Black Angus restaurant in Stockton on our first date. Luckily, I started to relax more as we conversed. I was usually shy around girls, but that was not the case with Adela. She was unique, unlike the other girls I had been with. It was as if we had known each other for many years. There was something about her eyes that made me feel at ease while simultaneously making me lose all my *sentidos*, or senses.

Our conversation flowed with ease until I noticed a change in her.

"Are you not feeling well? Would you like for me to take you home?" I asked like a total gentleman.

"No. Thank you. I'm fine," she replied.

"Are you sure? You don't seem well. Is it something I did, or said?"

"No. It's just that you're not like the other guys I've been with. I can already see you are special."

*"Special?"* I could not believe she used that word to describe me. I said, "Thank you. I think you're special too."

"Really?"

"Yes."

Adela looked at me in silence, or *silencio*, with her beautiful green eyes. It was not until much later that she confessed she was very nervous because she did not want to ruin her chances at a second date by saying or doing something wrong.

I did not see her again until our second date, which was two weeks later, because I had to go on a business trip to Kansas City. By this time, we spoke to each other with more confidence, or *confianza*.

"You know, José, I'm also from Michoacán. And my family is really supportive and close, just like yours. We're just trying to make it in life, like everyone else. Surely you know what I mean."

"Of course I do. It's hard for us first-generation kids to make it here in the U.S. But just remember, everything is possible."

"Even when the odds are against you and it is hard to believe that?" she asked in a saddened voice.

"Yes, Adelita, even when the odds are against you. Dreams do come true; you just have to believe wholeheartedly."

"Do you have dreams, José?"

"I do. Someday I'll tell you about them," I answered sincerely, as I took hold of her hand for the first time.

I looked up at the sky that night as I had done so many times before. This time, however, the stars did not make me think of my childhood; they made me think about Adela's eyes. The waning moon, which had accompanied me on my many trips down to La Piedad as a child, reminded me of her smile, and the night sky reminded me of her dark black hair.

I was starting to have these feelings I had never had before, and I realized that I was falling deeply in love with Adela. I did not know what to do next. *Should I ask her to be my girlfriend? If so, how? Is it too soon to ask? What would happen if she said no?* These were just some of the many *preguntas*, or questions, that ran through my mind. I could not stop thinking of my Adelita and her beautiful green eyes.

# CHAPTER 6

# He Who Perseveres Will Achieve

*The meaning of things lies not in the things themselves,*
*but in our attitude towards them.*

ANTOINE DE SAINT-EXUPÉRY (1900–1944)
FRENCH AUTHOR

Aside from the murder of my *tíos* in Stockton, the death, or *la muerte*, of my grandfather José was the most devastating event I had experienced thus far. I remember all the good times we spent together when I look at the photographs we took in La Piedad and in the fields of Northern California.

My *abuelo* closed his eyes in La Piedad for the last time in 1991. Many years of arduous labor finally took its toll on his body and soul. I do not like to remember him as an old man. Instead, I like to close my eyes and see him as the lively figure he was during my childhood years. His sweet laugh and tender, raspy voice will always be embedded in my memory.

My family and I hastily made arrangements to go to La Piedad to see him one last time, but when we arrived it was too late. He had passed away hours before we got there. We stayed for his wake and burial. I had never really understood why people were unable to bring themselves to look at their loved one's coffin being lowered into the ground; but on the day of my grandfather's funeral, I finally understood how people could feel that way. I had been to a few funerals and wakes in my life but never to one where the deceased meant so much to me.

*...And when I die, [I do not want] any light,*
*No crying, no mourning, or anything else,*
*Here, next to my cross, I only want peace...*

The lyrics of "The Wanderer," or "*El Andariego*," could be heard throughout the cemetery in unison with the chorus of the farewells. My family could not stop crying; no one could refrain from expressing their grief, including my normally strong and stoic father. There was not a single dry eye in sight. That night, my grandmother, doña Cleotilde—or Tilde, as everyone called her—was inconsolable. She cried to the point of having no more tears left to cry. During the ceremony, as the song continued, she looked up toward the heavens, and in a soft, weak voice said, "I miss you so much, my old, sweet man. So much that I'm going to die without you."

*...Only you, sweetheart, if you remember my love,*
*Cry one last tear for me,*
*Say a prayer for me in silence, and for God's sake,*
*Forget about me afterwards.*

After the funeral, I went back to Ticuítaco and stood in the same spot where he and I used to watch the golden sunset glisten off the water. Soon thereafter, we would start counting the first of the many stars and planets that brightened the view as the sky darkened. On this day, however, I looked up at the sky and reminisced about the times when my *abuelo* would tell me to wish upon a star.

"Make a wish, José," he would tell me.

On the night of my grandfather's funeral, I did just that: *"I wish that my grandfather José will always be proud of me, no matter what I do."* And it was at that moment when I realized that our loved one's body, or *cuerpo*, is the only thing that comes to rest for all of eternity, not his or her spirit; people are only gone when we stop thinking about them. There is no doubt in my mind that my *abuelo* is in Heaven, watching proudly over me and my own *familia*.

Hearing my *abuela* Tilde's plea, God must not have wanted her to experience such grief for too long. Months after my grandfather's death, her Alzheimer's rapidly accelerated and robbed her of her last memory. It was not long before she reunited with her soul mate, my *abuelo*.

They say that *tragedias*, or tragedies, come in threes, and this proved true for me. Shortly after the deaths of both my paternal grandparents came the passing of my maternal *abuela*, Chayo. It hurt me to not be able to attend her funeral. I was now working in the nuclear nonproliferation arena for Lawrence Livermore National Laboratory and was in the middle of a three-week international business trip in the heartland of the Russian Federation. Upon returning home, my mother told me that my *abuela* Chayo had succumbed to stomach cancer, a disease she did not know she had until it was too late to treat. But in the end, my mother said she passed peacefully. My only consolation was being able to visit her grave months later at the cemetery located in the outskirts of Ticuítaco.

After the passing of my *abuelos*, La Piedad and Ticuítaco ceased to be the special places they once were when my grandparents were alive. Even though we still have *tíos*, *tías*, and *primos* in La Piedad, my family and I gradually started to pull our roots from its soil.

The modest two-story brick house that my father finally finished was left empty. It was not until my father asked his sister, my *tía* Rosa, and her family to move into the house that a family finally enjoyed the fruits of my father's hard labor. To speak about our time in Michoacán today is like speaking about a distant memory. My family and I returned to Stockton, California, and slowly moved on with our lives.

I knew my grandfather would be proud of me if I accomplished the one thing I had always asked of the stars—to be an astronaut. I was not going to give up on my dream. I was determined to make it a reality. However, everything is much easier said than done.

To move forward with my story, I have to go back in time to my earlier days at the Lawrence Livermore National Laboratory. This laboratory had been my employer for the past four years, and it is safe to say that it was, and still is, one of the most prestigious places of employment for an engineer or scientist. The laboratory focuses on nuclear defense and energy research projects. For my first project, I was part of an elite team of scientists and engineers involved in the development of a nuclear pumped X-ray laser. This laser was to be developed and subsequently deployed into space as part of President Reagan's 1983 Strategic Defense Initiative (SDI), dubbed by the press as the "Star Wars" defense program. This program—clearly the result of the Cold War era—would serve as an orbiting defense shield that would have the capability of deactivating oncoming enemy missiles via a high-energy

X-ray pulse. This system was designed in the event that the Soviet Union launched an offensive nuclear first strike. It took years of intensive labor and sacrifice, not to mention many underground nuclear tests, to develop such a system. I was proud to have worked on this project, as it was something that had the ability to prevent the deaths of millions of innocent people.

## December 8, 1991: Dissolution of the U.S.S.R.

It was expected that one day the Union of Soviet Socialist Republics (U.S.S.R.), otherwise known as the Soviet Union, would cease to exist, and when that day came it made headlines around the world. Conversations everywhere turned into speculation over what our world leaders would do, especially after the fall of the Berlin Wall. What would happen to communism? To our economy? It was all that people could talk about around the water cooler at the laboratory.

> We, the republics of Belarus, the Russian Federation (RF), and Ukraine, as founding countries of the U.S.S.R., and signers of the treaty in 1922, hereinafter referred to as High Contracting Parties, declare that the U.S.S.R., as subject of international law and geopolitical, no longer exists.

Newspapers, radio programs, and television news networks ran stories about the above declaration, nonstop.

It was not long after the fall of the Soviet Union that expensive "Star Wars" defense programs, such as our own X-ray laser program, came up on the congressional budget's chopping block. There was no longer a need to complete the development of the space deployable X-ray laser defense system.

Most of my colleagues on the project quickly moved on to other projects within the Laboratory. Others, like me, stayed a little longer to ensure the proper closing and documentation of the program.

During this period I had time to contemplate the historical significance of Reagan's "Star Wars" programs. Though many did not agree with the United States of America's strategy of spending vast amounts of money on defense projects, this strategy took its toll on the Soviet Union. I credit the advances in defense shield projects such as our own X-ray laser as leading to the downfall of the former Soviet Union. In short, Reagan's strategy worked! My own conclusion leads me to believe that— in an effort to keep up with the Joneses—the Soviet Union dedicated the bulk of its budget to similar programs while paying less attention to their economy and internal infrastructure. As a result, the U.S.S.R. created the perfect social and economic storm that led to unrest and its eventual downfall.

We began to shut down the X-ray laser program and, as is typical with canceled programs, a lot of good work goes unused and subsequently gets mothballed. Within my own area of expertise, I felt our work and knowledge of X-ray transport analysis could be applied to other areas. The one question that started to linger in my mind was: *How could we utilize, to our advantage, the insight gathered from work on the X-ray laser?* My boss and mentor, Clint Logan, could not have agreed more. Both he and I pondered this constantly, even on our days off. We were certain that we could find something that would benefit from this extensive research and development. It was as if we had an answer but did not know the question.

"It's a shame. We worked tirelessly to develop this system and we didn't even get to see it in action," said Clint.

"I know, but thank God we don't live in an environment where we feel we need it. I'll take that trade-off any day!"

"Yes, you're right, José, but we were so close…," he said, looking away in the hope that someone would overhear him and order us to continue working on the X-ray laser program. He paused before exclaiming, "Wait a minute! I just thought of how we can use our knowledge from the system for something else."

"Really?" I asked excitedly.

"Yes. We can use our X-ray modeling tools in the area of medical imaging. We know how X-rays interact with matter, and our models can be used in the energy regimes similar to those used for human imaging."

Clint, being a seasoned researcher, was always a few steps ahead of me, and this particular instance was no different. Clint was on to something significant. We had many ideas on how the technology could be beneficial, but none proved worthy of further exploration. We wanted to identify an area where we could have a significant impact. Also, we had to find a funding source that would pay for our work. The U.S. Department of Energy (DOE) funds most of the efforts at Lawrence Livermore National Laboratory, but their charter is in energy and national defense.

Clint decided that mammography was the best match to both our skills and the tools we had developed. We also had personal motives for improving mammography. The wife of our leader in the X-ray laser program had been diagnosed with breast cancer, and I had just lost a young friend to the disease. On many occasions, I served as an interpreter for my twenty-eight-year-old friend and her husband as she underwent treatment for her cancer. I was astonished to learn that eventually one in eight women in the United States acquires this horrible disease.

The machine we had in mind would be used for screening women in order to detect breast cancer as early as possible. It was well established that early detection saves lives. We learned that the taking and interpreting of mammograms had not changed much in twenty years. Images were captured on film, and radiologists studied the films on a light box. We believed it was feasible to capture the image electronically and to use a computer to help the radiologist identify suspicious areas. It was also clear to us that improvements could be made in the X-ray source. We made our arguments within Lawrence Livermore National Laboratory and were awarded a small grant to pursue these ideas.

If we were ever going to make an impact in the health of women, we had to find an established industrial partner. Clint wrote to every manufacturer of mammography equipment. Fischer Imaging of Denver, Colorado, responded positively, so we quickly formed an alliance with Morgan Nields and his team. Fischer had ideas that aligned with our own. Together we sought funding from the National Institutes of Health and from the U.S. Army. We were rejected.

Fischer began an internal R&D project to develop their conceptual design. Clint and I brainstormed every day, everywhere. We sketched great ideas on paper, whiteboards, napkins, Post-its, and anything we could write on that was near at hand. We modeled X-ray transport through tissue, and we had a concept for an X-ray source that would be more efficient and tunable to different breast sizes and compositions. This system would reduce the radiation dosage to the patient and produce a superior image.

Once we settled on electronic detection, similar to what is used in digital cameras, it was apparent that light tables would be replaced with high-resolution computer monitors. Hazardous waste chemicals used for film processing would be eliminated as well. Immediate access to the image would eliminate callbacks for patients because of a bad exposure. Now the radiologist would just adjust contrast and brightness on the monitor. The image could be transmitted to a remote site for consultation or for interpretation, and computer-aided diagnosis would become practical.

Just as Clint and I had exhausted our internal grant, the DOE sent out a call for proposals that seemed ready-made for us. The DOE was also concerned that laboratory technology developed for defense would be lost. They created the Cooperative Research and Development Agreement (CRADA) program. This program provided funding that allowed researchers from national laboratories, such as Lawrence Livermore National Laboratory, to partner with U.S. companies and transfer unclassified technology in order to improve U.S. technical competitiveness. This specific call for proposals focused on medical technology. In collaboration with Fischer Imaging, we submitted a proposal. Award selections would be made six months from the date of our submission.

Knowing this, I decided to take advantage of the laboratory's continuing education program and enrolled at the University of California at Santa Barbara's (UCSB) PhD program.

My previous graduate advisor at UCSB, Dr. Sanjit Mitra, extended an open invitation for me to join his research team as part of UCSB's PhD engineering program. In essence, I was at a crossroads in my career. I did not want to get assigned to another program at the lab, as I was certain that in six months we would obtain funding for the digital mammography project. Hence, continuing my education while I waited seemed like a smart approach. The logic was simple: I would enroll and take graduate courses with an emphasis in biomedicine while waiting for an answer from the DOE proposal. If successful, I would return to Lawrence Livermore National Laboratory and use what I learned at UCSB in the design of a new digital mammography device. If we were unsuccessful in obtaining funding, I would stay at UCSB and finish my PhD. I talked this plan over with Clint, who was not only my boss but also my mentor. He agreed that this was a win-win situation for all parties involved.

After almost a full school year at UCSB, we finally heard from the DOE that our project was indeed selected for funding! Three years of hard work—both at Lawrence Livermore National Laboratory and Fischer Imaging—commenced, and everyone involved was as dedicated as could be to this project. It promised to produce a vital piece of equipment for the medical community, and the laboratory was pleased to have partnered with Fischer Imaging in the creation of it.

## A Taste of Rejection

In early 1992, when I was twenty-nine years old, I called the National Aeronautics and Space Administration (NASA) to ask about the requirements to become an astronaut. I was hoping to make what was a far-fetched dream for many a reality for myself. Here were the requirements:

- Career in a technical field or medicine: ✓
- Five years experience: ✓
- Highly desirable: Graduate degree: ✓

Nothing prevented me from applying since I met all of the basic requirements. Hence, I decided to contact NASA. Much to my surprise, the main operator put me in contact with the Astronaut Selection Office. As part of the first step in the application process, the Astronaut Selection Office sent me a twelve-page application. I promptly filled it out and mailed it back to NASA.

Shortly after I mailed off my application, I received a confirmation postcard that read, "Thank you for submitting your application. We will contact you in the event there is further interest in your application." Not a day went by that I did not check my mail since I knew they were going to select a new class of astronauts that very same year. I finally received a letter in the mail four months after having received the acknowledgment of my application. It read: *"Thank you for your interest in NASA. At the moment, there are many qualified applicants applying for astronaut positions with NASA. Unfortunately, we cannot invite you to an interview for this selection cycle. We encourage you to continue applying for future selection cycles."*

Disappointment was my initial feeling after reading the letter denying me the opportunity to become an astronaut.

Thankfully, my girlfriend and soon to be wife, Adelita, was there to console me.

"Don't worry, you are very young and have many years ahead of you, José. Just reapply. Your opportunity will come, you'll see," she said reassuringly.

Her words gave me hope and made me feel a lot better. I then started asking myself over and over: *When will my opportunity come?* I had no other choice but to continue with my life until the application process reopened the following year. In the meantime, I had to focus on my other responsibilities instead of spinning my wheels trying to figure out why I was rejected.

Back at the laboratory, news began to spread that our former boss's wife was losing her battle against breast cancer. Unfortunately, it was discovered too late; with our boss at her side, she passed away peacefully. From that moment on, ensuring the continued development of the full-field digital mammography device for the early detection of breast cancer seemed like a poignantly indispensable task. The phrase "to save a life" never had so much meaning to me after the death of my boss's wife and of my friend. It was clear to me that we not only had the opportunity but also the responsibility to use our technology and knowledge to quickly complete the development of a potentially lifesaving device. Today, I am convinced that due to our contributions in the field of medical imaging, many women are still alive because they benefited from the use of digital imaging that we had a hand in advancing.

We worked with some of the most renowned doctors in both our community and the country at the University of California at San Francisco to better understand how they diagnosed radiographs. We learned that the doctors looked for early possible precursors to breast cancer such as microcalcifications, asymmetric distortions, stellate, and circumscribed lesions. I emphasize *possible* precursors because even if a patient's mammogram contained such indications, it did not necessarily mean that he or she had breast cancer. Many other tests are needed, including procedures such as ultrasound and needle core biopsies, before an accurate diagnosis can be made.

After doing most of our analysis in the design of this device and while Fischer Imaging was building several test devices, efficacy tests and studies were being designed at Fischer. Food and Drug Administration (FDA) approval is a necessary step for any new medical imaging device before it can be put to clinical use. Many months of adjusting, studying, testing, and demonstrating the device went by before Fischer Imaging could finally say, "It's ready to go through the FDA approval process." The three years spent developing the device seemed to have gone by fast in comparison to the long wait we endured for the FDA approval. Nevertheless, we were excited to unveil our creation.

"Full-field digital mammography was developed with X-ray laser technology. It functions just like today's digital camera. It captures a mammogram image and transfers it immediately to a computer where a doctor can effectively analyze and detect early signs of breast cancer. Furthermore, the computer can be programmed to assist the doctor in highlighting areas of interest," Clint explained, as Fischer was preparing to put the device on the market.

Our project was a complete success. Our digital mammography project became the poster child of the DOE as

they touted the benefits of applying technology originating
from national defense programs to more peaceful applications.
The medical community saw the potential of the device and
lauded our efforts. Other medical imaging companies developed their own versions of digital screening mammography
units. In fact, GE was the first company that obtained FDA
approval for clinical use of the imaging device. We took this
as a compliment and were happy that the medical community
was exploiting the benefits of high-resolution digital imaging
technology.

Soon thereafter, the solid-state detector technology had
advanced enough that larger area digital imagers for applications such as chest X-rays started to show up in the medical
imaging community. Now when new radiological facilities are
designed, they do not even contain a film processor because of
the advancements in imaging technologies.

I can honestly say that this is the one project that has brought
me the most satisfaction. My work in helping to advance the
early detection of breast cancer—which also enhanced both
patient and practitioner care—taught me an important lesson:
there is more than one star in the sky and more than one goal
and purpose in life.

I continued to work tirelessly on other projects until my
wedding on May 30, 1992.


Adela and I dated for more than two years before we decided
to get married. We were not in any rush to tie the knot even
though we knew we were meant to be together. I remember the first time I thought of how I would ask her to marry
me. As I pondered how I would ask this important question,

I broke into a cold sweat. I was not worried about building up the courage to ask the question, but I was worried about coming up with the perfect words for—and most romantic way of—asking the question. Would I propose in a restaurant in front of a lot of strangers? Should I post it on a billboard or maybe a giant sign towed in the air by an airplane? After much thought, I decided this was a moment that only she and I should enjoy. I planned to take her out to a nice dinner and then park in an isolated area where I could pop the question. So that is what I did.

After Adela and I had a great dinner date, I convinced her that I wanted to drive to a nice isolated area where we could do some stargazing. I told her that I would like to point out some of the many constellations to her that were not readily visible in the city due to the bright lights. Shortly after arriving and turning off the car engine, I reached into the glove compartment and retrieved a diamond engagement ring I had carefully stored. The diamond on the engagement ring, as Adela now likes to tease me, was so small that it needed a magnifying glass attached to it so it could be seen.

Though I had carefully prepared a speech, only five simple words flowed from my lips: "Adelita, will you marry me?"

"Yes," she said in a sweet, nervous voice as she tried to catch her breath.

Shortly thereafter, we embraced and gave each other a very long, passionate kiss. Then we started to talk about our future together. We feverishly began planning the wedding, and we discussed how we would inform our relatives of our engagement. I was just so overwhelmed by my emotions, and I could not help but think about how my life was about to change.

From that moment on, it was no longer going to be just me. I had found a soul mate who would stand by me and be there for me. Adelita always had the right solutions to my problems. She has been—and always will be—the love of my life and my best friend.

In my culture it is tradition that once a couple decides to marry, the groom visits the bride's parents with his own father or a priest to ask for the bride's hand in marriage. I decided to bring my father along. As a result, my father and my future father-in-law initially enjoyed engaging in some small talk. Shortly thereafter, my father grew more serious before addressing my future father-in-law.

"Don Aniceto, as you know, these two kids have been dating. My son here tells me he would like to marry your daughter."

To which Don Aniceto replied half-kiddingly and with a smile as he said, "*Sí*, I thought this would be the reason of your visit. My daughter is certainly old enough to know whether this is what she wants to do. However, I must warn you, José, that she is a bit hardheaded. You are going to have to deal with this. I just don't want you to come back and say I didn't warn you!"

I nodded my head and acknowledged his half-joking and half-serious comment.

Having completed this visit, Adela and I were officially engaged. Now we could plan the wedding. My sister and parents wanted a big wedding for us. However, Adela and I were a bit more conservative, and we opted to have a small, traditional wedding.

Six months after we got engaged, we exchanged vows in a

traditional Catholic ceremony in Lodi, California, at St. Anne's Catholic Church. On the way to pick up Adela, the limousine got lost and caused her to arrive forty-five minutes late to the wedding. Talk about being a nervous groom! I was starting to fear that she had changed her mind! Upon her arrival, Father Joseph Illo explained to us that another wedding was going to start soon, so our wedding ceremony would have to be performed rather quickly. What a chaotic experience!

After the wedding, we held a reception in the backyard of the house my parents and I shared. We were so pleased that our friends and relatives were present to celebrate our joyous occasion. The garden reception was accompanied by live mariachi musicians, and we all enjoyed the traditional dish served at Mexican weddings of *mole poblano*. The night ended with a truly Mexican tradition—the fusion of tequila and music!

When I look at the photos of my wedding, or *boda*, I cannot help but be captivated all over again by my wife's beauty. To this day, I have never seen such beauty in another woman—this is something I wish I would have told her more during our first twenty years of marriage. However, it is never too late to tell a woman how much you love her and, just as I am completely committed to her, I am committed to telling her how passionately I care for her for the next twenty years and beyond.

"I knew you were the one for me when I first saw you," I whispered in her ear, as we danced our first dance as husband and wife.

"I knew you were the one for me when I saw you for the first time too," she confessed with a smile.

We escaped for a brief moment out of the presence of our

guests in order to look up at the stars in the night sky. I looked up at them and then at her face; I realized that looking into her eyes offered a sight even more radiant than that of looking into the heaven of stars above. She rested her head on my shoulder and we continued dancing together as she whispered the lyrics from an Armando Manzanero song into my ear: *"I realized I became full of life the day I met you..."*

For our honeymoon, or *luna de miel,* we flew to Spain, a country we both thought we would enjoy. It was in Madrid that we spent our first night together, alone, as husband and wife. We joyously spent the subsequent two weeks traveling in a rental car throughout one of the most beautiful and most romantic countries in the world. We visited cities like Madrid, Costa del Sol, Toledo, Córdoba, and the location of the world's fair—Sevilla.

In Córdoba, I quickly learned that giving my wife wine on an empty stomach was not a good idea. As we waited for our food in a restaurant called *el Caballo Rojo,* or the Red Horse, we both drank wine on empty stomachs. I quickly noticed the effect it was having on my wife; she started to giggle more and thought everything I said was funny. This was the first time I had ever seen Adela slightly intoxicated, and I was glad to see that it made her demeanor cheerful and festive!

Once our two-week honeymoon was over, I landed back in reality with the goal of becoming an astronaut still on my mind. Another year passed, so once again, I filled out the twelve-page application and waited for an answer. Then, after four months of waiting to hear whether or not I had been accepted, I received another rejection letter with words to the effect of: "Don't call us, we'll call you." This process of applying and being rejected repeated itself every year while I continued working at the laboratory. Whenever I received a rejection letter from NASA, I would remind myself that there is more than just one star and one goal in life. I had no other choice but to move forward with my life. Adelita's positive influence helped me develop a healthy balance between work and family; thus, I could safely avoid being consumed with the notion of trying to become an astronaut. She helped me cope with NASA's rejections while encouraging me to sustain my dream. I still wanted to become an astronaut, but I also wanted to live—and enjoy—my life on my way to becoming one.

A little over a year and a half into our marriage, Adela announced she was pregnant with our first child. We experienced our first pregnancy with all the excitement of first-time parents—and with all the nerves, too! As the pregnancy progressed, we read everything we could on pregnancy and parenting. Since we made the decision not to find out the sex of the baby, I busily converted our extra bedroom into a nursery with neutral colors.

The excitement surrounding our firstborn continued through the delivery, which occurred on August 17, 1994. Witnessing the birth of my first child was truly an amazing and emotional experience! I still remember how the tears of joy gleefully trickled down my cheeks as the doctor announced that we were the parents of a healthy baby boy. I was astounded by how wonderful it felt to know that I played a part in creating this new life that I had just witnessed enter the world. Holding my son for the first time while standing next to my lovely wife only made it harder to hold back the tears that, by this point, had begun to flow down my face.

We decided to name him Julio Andres, after my mother, Julia. I did not know if we would have another baby—let alone a girl—so I decided to honor my mother by naming my firstborn after her.

Once we completed the digital mammography project, I was promoted to lead the Chemistry and Materials Analysis Group within the Engineering Directorate's Defense Science Engineering Division. This was the group I originally worked with as an intern while at the University of the Pacific. The group provided engineering technical support to the laboratory's Chemistry Directorate. As the leader of this group, I learned many things and picked up both management and motivational skills; I applied these newfound skills to a broad range of technical personnel while I was managing tasks to ensure they remained on budget and on schedule. However, I longed to get back into the technical arena and still considered myself too young to take a permanent plunge into the world of management.

After three years of leading this group, I saw a great opportunity to get back into a hands-on technical project. The Department of Energy was forming the High Enriched Uranium (HEU) Transparency Program and requesting the involvement of personnel from national laboratories to work on developing technical transparency measures as a major component of the program. These measures would be used in the execution of a highly enriched uranium purchase agreement between the United States Department of Energy and the Russian Federation's Ministry of Atomic Energy.

This program was one of several solutions jointly developed with the Russians to address the issue of what to do with

Cold War–era Russian scientists and with weapons-grade nuclear material; the project was necessitated by Russia's dismantlement of excess nuclear weapons. The purchase agreement called for the Russian Federation to sell more than twelve metric tons of highly enriched uranium to the United States over a twenty-year period. However, Russia did not want to sell the uranium to the U.S. as weapons-grade material and instead wanted to chemically down-blend the material to be sold as fuel-grade material. The U.S. was amenable to this compromise because upon receiving the material, they would convert it to fuel pellets and assemble it into nuclear fuel rods to be resold to the nuclear reactor industry as fuel.

It was a win-win situation for all. The U.S. would ensure that excess weapons-grade nuclear material would not fall into the hands of rogue organizations or nations; meanwhile, Russia would achieve the goal of keeping its nuclear scien tists gainfully employed. The only concern was that the U.S. government wanted assurances that the fuel-grade uranium that Russia provided actually originated from the dismantlement of nuclear weapons. The U.S. was paying a premium for this fuel-grade uranium and it would be tempting for the Russians to utilize their thousands of centrifuges to enrich natural mined uranium, thus defeating the spirit of such an agreement.

I joined a group of engineers and scientists who formed the technical arm of the collaboration between the State Department and the Department of Energy during the Geneva-based negotiations with the Russian counterparts of these departments. In these meetings, we were able to develop and negotiate mutually satisfactory agreements that would allow a certain level of transparency previously not present in the dealings between the two nations. Furthermore, these negotiations gave the U.S. government the necessary assurances that all uranium received under this purchase agreement originated from dismantled Russian nuclear weapons.

In the process, we formed close ties and established solid relationships with our Russian colleagues. In addition, the national laboratories had the ultimate responsibility of implementing the technical aspects of the agreement. Thus, over the next five years, my team traveled across parts of the Russian Siberian countryside—to various nuclear materials process facilities on more than twenty occasions—where my team members and I installed monitoring equipment in accordance with the agreement. Overall, it was a great experience that helped establish a strong bond between both countries. I thought it was a great irony that I started working at the laboratory on a Star Wars project to protect the U.S. from a Russian missile attack, and then I went on to form part of a team whose objective was to unite both countries. I was now tasked with helping the Russians dispose of their excess nuclear materials as a result of their nuclear weapons reduction efforts. The latter project proved to be highly successful and is still being implemented to this day.

On the home front, Adela announced that she was once again pregnant. It had been only a few months since the arrival of our first child, Julio. We knew we wanted to have a second child, we just did not know it would happen so soon. Our memory was still fresh from the first pregnancy, allowing us to approach the second pregnancy with a more relaxed attitude. This time, we even decided to inquire about the sex of the baby during the normal ultrasound checkups. We were happy to find out that our second child would be a girl. *Perfect!* I remember saying to myself. I was excited that my wife and I would soon have a pair—a baby boy and a baby girl! It seemed that all was well in the world.

During Adela's pregnancy with our second child, I was traveling extensively to the former Soviet Union for Lawrence Livermore National Laboratory and the U.S. Department of Energy. My new job was very satisfying and I enjoyed all of the traveling—with a few notable exceptions. Unfortunately, an important meeting I had to attend was taking place three weeks before Adela's due date. Adela convinced me to attend my important meeting, as I would be back in plenty of time before the delivery. As luck would have it, I found out while I was still in Siberia that Adela had gone into labor and given birth to our baby girl. We named our daughter Karina Isabel because Adela thought she had the most precious-looking face, and the name Karina seemed to best reflect that sentiment.

My experiences on these twenty or so trips to the Siberian countryside were both incredible and very exhausting. It takes more than twelve hours to get to Russia, where the winter cold pierces through the bones as soon as one steps foot outside the airplane. Moscow is surrounded by nothing but beauty, but my final destination was not this city with its delicate balance of old-world charm and a cosmopolitan way of life. I would be continuing on to the Siberian countryside—the area known for its limitless birch forest and cold, snowy weather. My colleagues and I would arrive and stay in small, "closed" cities where few foreigners are allowed to travel. Here I was exposed to what I consider to be the real Russia. In these closed cities, many people worked for government-run facilities, such as the nuclear materials facilities I was visiting. Most, if not all, supplemented their diets by planting vegetables next to their dachas, or summer log cabin homes. The homes they lived in resembled their way of life—simple and austere. It reminded me of Ticuítaco, Michoacán, in Mexico, which was so far away, yet so close in many ways.

During one of my trips to Russia, I came to an important *conclusión*: Nothing in life happens or is accomplished purely by chance. Goals and dreams are realized through planning, perseverance, and hard work. As I was leaning my head against the window of the state-owned car that was taking us to our hotel, I thought of how my childhood dream had evolved with my graduation from college and my work at one of the most prestigious laboratories in the United States and the world. It was because I worked tirelessly that I could see the transformative effect that my *sueño* had on shaping each outcome in my life.

The three projects that I worked on during my first twelve years at the Lawrence Livermore National Laboratory helped me come one step closer to my goal of becoming an astronaut. It was the knowledge, or *conocimiento*, that I gained of X-ray lasers, materials, and nondestructive testing that gave me the background and experience I thought was necessary to make me a viable candidate for the NASA astronaut program.

My time working alongside the Russians was also useful because there had been talk between the U.S. and Russia of creating an International Space Station (ISS). My job working in the field in Russia allowed me to take Russian-language courses through the laboratory. Three years of these courses helped me to hold my own in basic conversations, though I was still far from being fluent. While I might not have been able to negotiate treaties in Russian, I was able to order beer at the bar and ask for directions on the subway.

I also focused on bettering my physical strength and health because astronauts are susceptible to rigorous training and medical exams before blasting off into space. I ran a marathon almost every year I applied to NASA with the exception of the year that I was finally selected to become a member of an astronaut class. Little did I know at the time I began this routine that this would mean I would end up running eleven marathons!

Additionally, I took flying lessons at the Tracy Municipal Airport and obtained my SCUBA certification through the laboratory's Vaqueros del Mar SCUBA diving club. These were skills I suspected (and later confirmed) were indispensable for an astronaut to have. I learned many things during the time I spent enhancing my skill sets, but—above all—I learned that patience really is a virtue; it is simply the best tool to have in one's toolbox when learning something new.

The first time I ever flew on my own was after completing about thirty hours of flight school at the Tracy Municipal Airport. I was elated with the knowledge that I would finally live my childhood dream of flying even higher than a bird; I did so on a Cessna 152, as I soared above the town of Tracy, just west of Stockton. My instructor allowed me to fly solo and I experienced an inexplicable sensation. I felt like a young bird that was learning how to fly for the first time without the aid of his mother. I flew at about five thousand feet above ground, dodging the few clouds that were out that day. It was something magical. I could not believe I had the ability to control a plane on my own and, in doing so, control my destiny. Now I understood why aviators love to fly any chance they get.

After landing on the runway, I was filled with a sense of empowerment. My chest swelled as I thought to myself: *If I was able to learn how to fly, then perhaps I am ready to finally reach the stars.* From that moment on, I wanted to fast-track my selection into the NASA astronaut program. I convinced myself that it would only be a matter of time.

A little more than a year after our second child, Karina, joined our family, my wife and I found out that we would once again bring a life into the world. By this time, we felt we were experts in the pregnancy department; accordingly, we took the news in stride. What I did know was that if we were going to have three kids, we probably would balance things out by having a fourth. Since we already had a baby boy and a baby girl, we really did not have any preference as to whether our third child would be a boy or a girl. The ultrasound indicated the child would be a boy.

Up to this point, Adela, our children, and I were still living in the same place we were living when we got married. It was a single-wide mobile home I bought and put on the property that my parents and I owned. Having bought the property with my father a few years before I got married, Adela and I really could not afford another mortgage, hence the mobile home solution. However, as the years passed by and as my family grew, I knew there was a need to move into something bigger. Luckily, Adela, who worked as a pharmacy technician, and I had the financial ability to do so by this time. Adela and I made the decision to purchase a fixer-upper in Stockton located on Walnut Street near my alma mater, the University of the Pacific. As I fixed up the house, I estimated that it would be ready shortly after the arrival of our third child.

By this time, I was the program manager of the HEU Transparency Program at Lawrence Livermore National Laboratory. On June 9, 1997—the day that my third child arrived—I was working on the appraisal input and salary increases of my group members. It was an important meeting, as I was recommending the proposed raises of each HEU program member. During the middle of this process, I received a note saying that my wife was on her way to the hospital because she was going into labor. I had approximately one hour left in the meeting and I lived about an hour's drive from work. Since I figured my wife would be in labor for a while, I decided to wait until the end of my meeting before making my way to the hospital in Lodi, California. This turned out to be a very, very bad decision on my part. Halfway through my drive to the hospital, I received a call from my mother telling me to slow down and drive carefully as the new baby and its mother were doing fine. I could not believe I missed—for the second time—the birth of one of my babies!

Upon arriving at Lodi Memorial Hospital, I could not bring myself to enter my wife's room empty-handed. I quickly slipped into the hospital's gift shop. I bought a beautiful flower arrangement for my wife and a balloon bouquet for the baby. I remember picking out the best flower arrangement for my Adelita. I also chose the most impressive balloon bouquet for the baby; the largest of the balloons read "Congratulations! It's a Boy!" This, I thought to myself, would certainly get me out of the doghouse for missing the actual delivery.

Upon entering the recovery room, Adela looked at me with this very stern, yet loving smile.

"You're pathetic!" she mumbled as she stared at the balloon bouquet. "Come and meet your new daughter!"

*New daughter!* I thought. "But...but the doctor said it was boy!"

After a moment of laughter, she said, "Well, the doctor isn't always right!"

We had a good laugh, and I was able to meet my second daughter, Vanessa Adelita. I was adamant about naming one of our daughters after my lovely wife, but the most my wife would agree to was using her name as one of the girls' middle names. Adela was not very fond of her name, and she did not want to burden one of our children with the name. I, of course, felt differently. Vanessa Adelita, like our first daughter, Karina Isabel, was a beautiful and precious baby.

It was now 1998, and the HEU Transparency Program was in its full implementation phase. The U.S. was buying low-enriched uranium while receiving assurances that it originated as high-enriched uranium from Russian dismantled nuclear weapons. This was, in no small way, thanks to the monitoring trips to the Siberian uranium processing facilities that I had been a part of for years by this time.

The next issue to be addressed at the Department of Energy headquarters was how to help the Russians safeguard the weapons-grade material they decided to keep. The Russian Federation's nuclear weapons reduction efforts practically forced the U.S. to devise a plan for how to handle excess nuclear material on Russian soil. Shortly thereafter, I was offered a two-year federal government appointment at the Department of Energy headquarters in Washington, D.C. I accepted the position to be part of a team that formed the Material Protection, Control and Accountability (MPC&A) program. The MPC&A program's charter was to help the Russian Federation improve their safeguard methodologies for nuclear materials. This was accomplished by providing technical and fiscal resources to each of the individual sites containing nuclear materials.

My family and I began to prepare for the move to Washington. I also started thinking about the years NASA denied my admission into their training program: 1992, 1993, 1994, 1995, 1996, and 1997. Right before we left for Washington to start my two-year assignment, NASA finally called offering me the invitation I had been waiting for my entire life!

The person on the phone informed me that out of more than 4,000 applicants, only 300 were selected for a closer look at their applications. Out of those 300 candidates, only 100 were selected to continue on to the final round of the selection process, and I was one of them. I was also informed that I had to spend a full week on-site for a series of in-depth medical and psychological exams, aptitude tests, and interviews. This news, though I had been waiting for it all my life, paralyzed me. I was unable to feel my legs or think clearly. I was in shock, stunned by disbelief that I was one step closer to finally reaching my dream after six years of blatant rejection.

There was nothing that could stop the adrenaline from running through my veins. My childhood dream was finally going to be a reality. Soon, I would be able to fly higher than any bird and surpass all the clouds in the sky to be among the stars in the heavens. Everything seemed like it was going according to plan, or so I thought.

It was not long before the other finalists and I arrived at the Johnson Space Center in Houston, Texas. As I drove through the main entrance, I saw an unused Saturn 5 rocket on display. We were later told this rocket would have been part of the Apollo 18 mission had the program not been abruptly canceled. The Saturn 5 was the exact type of rocket that had launched my imagination into thinking about outer space during my childhood, when I saw Apollo II blast off and then land on the Moon. For me, staring at the Saturn 5 and seeing it up close was surreal; it was as if a relic of science fiction was suspended in reality before my eyes.

We, the finalists, were placed in a conference room where the astronaut selection manager, Duane Ross, explained what we would be doing during our weeklong stay. He informed us that we were the third group of 20 candidates and that two more groups would be visiting the Johnson Space Center in the coming weeks. The purpose of our extensive exams was to help determine whether we met the medical requirements for a flight assignment. Of the 100 finalists interviewed, only 10 to 18 would be selected to become astronauts. Before Duane let us go, he informed us about some of the NASA space centers located in various sites across the U.S.

"There are ten space centers in the U.S., and each one specializes in something different. Here at Johnson, we dedicate ourselves to human spaceflight training; so if you are selected, you are expected to move and live here in the Houston area. Including contractors, we employ about eight thousand people and have simulators that our astronauts use for training. The

Kennedy Space Center (KSC) is where the space shuttles live. KSC owns the space shuttles and prepares them for every launch. The Ames Research Center, which is located in San Jose, California, is a computational-oriented center that is responsible for computer equipment, simulation, and testing. At the Marshall Center, located in Huntsville, Alabama, we have our propulsion systems. Both the Jet Propulsion Laboratory in Pasadena and the Goddard Space Flight Center in Maryland control our unmanned rovers and satellites. I'll stop now. I just wanted to mention a few before showing you around," Duane Ross said as we exited the conference room.

Each finalist spent eight to ten hours a day at NASA going through various medical exams. The exams performed on us tested our eyes, hearing, and blood, as well as urine. In addition, echocardiograms and electrocardiograms were performed on us. These exams were designed to detect any abnormalities, and each was performed meticulously. On average, about 20 out of the 100 finalists would be medically disqualified, thus leaving only 80 to compete for the coveted positions.

Each interview group of twenty aspiring astronauts formed a strong bond. We spent the week together going through one medical test after another, one tour after another, and exchanging our interview experiences with the astronaut recommendation panel. We even ate dinner together every evening. The stories of the other nineteen individuals were truly amazing. Some were military test pilots, others were helicopter pilots, still others were medical doctors, while the rest were engineers and scientists. All the candidates boasted résumés full of impressive accomplishments and very distinguished careers, making it clear to me why it had taken so long to get to this point. NASA looks for the best of the best; the competition was stiff among extremely well-prepared individuals who shared similar dreams. All the candidates exchanged e-mails and phone numbers, so we were able to keep in touch afterward. After all, we shared the same dream and were well aware that only a few of us would be chosen to advance.

Once we were all back home there were many conjectures, deductions, and expectations being made on the Internet as to whom NASA would pick. The pool of qualified candidates shrunk each day. Those who volunteered that they had been medically disqualified helped others—who kept a sort of scorecard—to keep track of the shrinking pool of candidates.

In addition, there were many messages from outsiders showing their support. They too were glued to the news, waiting to hear who was selected. At that point, I began to refer to the Internet correspondence as "the Cyber Soap Opera"; there was no better way to describe the drama-inducing environment where competing characters vied for their desires, allowing some to come out on top while leaving others desperate, emotional, and heartbroken.

The only list that truly mattered was the official list that NASA would soon issue. I had gone from being one of the 4,000 applicants, to the pool of 300 semifinalists, to one of the 100 finalists. Then I had passed all medical exams to be within the likely 80 remaining finalists. It was not until I learned that a federal agent, on the behalf of NASA, had paid a visit to my family and friends that I discovered I was on that short list of 40 remaining finalists!

My family and close friends were as excited as I was, if not more so. They even started celebrating my accomplishment.

*You did it, José! Congratulations! ¡Felicidades!* Their enthusiasm led me to believe that I was one of the chosen finalists; however, that would not be the case.

Duane Ross called and gave me the news, "José, thank you for your interest in our program. Unfortunately, you were not selected in this interview cycle. We encourage you to continue applying as we will be selecting future classes."

After years of applying and being denied, as well as being so close to actually being chosen to become an astronaut, the only thing they could tell me was, "Thank you for your interest." I was disappointed. I could not believe my dream was so close to coming true only to be shattered by a quick telephone call.

But wait, there was more. Duane Ross continued the phone conversation and said, "José, if you are interested, we would like to offer you a position as an engineer here at NASA-Johnson Space Center. However, this does not guarantee that you will be interviewed, let alone selected, during the next selection cycle. If you are interested in applying to become an astronaut, we suggest you get more operations experience, and we believe you can gain this type of experience and knowledge here at NASA."

I did not know what to think at that moment, and it was certainly not wise to accept a position without thinking through all the ramifications to my family and myself. I responded by asking for a few days to think about the offer.

By the time I got the final word that I was not to be part of the 1998 class of NASA astronauts, I was in Washington, D.C., and I was deep in my work with the MPC&A program. No one in the office dared to speak or ask me about anything for a couple of days after the announcement as they did not know how I was going to react. I even thought about never applying to NASA again. I gazed up at the stars in the night sky with a sense of hopelessness that night. "I will never reach my dream."

"What's wrong, José?" asked Adelita when she saw me crumple the rejection letter that had finally arrived in the mail confirming Duane Ross's call of a few days back.

"Nothing. Leave it alone," I said to her.

"Leave it? It doesn't belong on the floor."

I shrugged my shoulders because I did not care anymore.

"José, answer me. This is your dream. Why are you throwing it away?"

"Adelita, don't make things more complicated for me, please. I have a good job and I love what I do here at DOE and back home at the laboratory. What else do I need? They think highly of me and that's why they transferred me here to Washington. Do you know why they did that?"

"No. Why?"

"Because they are probably going to promote me to a higher position as soon as I get back to California."

"And is that a good enough reason for you to throw away your dream of becoming an astronaut?"

I did not answer her.

"Don't start making excuses," said Adela with an energy I had never seen in her before. She continued with vigor: "You told me that everything is possible if we truly believe it. You remember? This may not be the year you get accepted to NASA as an astronaut, but there is always next year. You're going to fill out that twelve-page application once again next year, and the year after that, until you get selected. You understand? You shouldn't give up; it's not like you. If you give up now, you will have to live with not knowing what would have happened had you not quit. If you are never going to be an astronaut, let it be because they reject you and not because you gave up trying."

I did not say one word after that. I knew she was right. I felt very blessed to have married a woman who demonstrated so much compassion and offered encouragement during the times I needed it the most. Because of that conversation, I decided to continue chasing my childhood dream.

Adelita answered the telephone one Saturday morning.

"Pepe, it's for you," she said as she handed me the phone.

"Who is it?" I asked.

"You are not going to believe me, but it's someone from NASA," she whispered, as she covered the phone with one hand before handing it to me.

"Hello?"

It was Duane Ross, the astronaut selection manager, from the Johnson Space Center in Houston. He wanted to know if I was going to accept the engineering position. After all, it was a great opportunity. However, Lawrence Livermore National Laboratory had just sent me to work in the nation's capital and it didn't seem right to suddenly quit after the lab had gone through the expense of relocating my family and me to Maryland. I also could not deny that I was confronted with an amazing opportunity to work directly with NASA. I was driving myself crazy thinking of what to do because I did not want to regret my decision afterward. Needless to say, I did not sleep that night.

The first thing I did Monday morning was call NASA to inform them of my decision.

"Hello. This is José Hernández. I would like to thank you for offering me an engineering position, but I'm afraid I cannot accept it."

When they inquired as to why I was declining their offer, I explained to them that I could not possibly leave my position representing the Lawrence Livermore National Laboratory at the U.S. Department of Energy. I explained the situation and how I felt it was very important to keep my two-year commitment to the laboratory. Luckily, they understood my situation and told me that perhaps I would be chosen as an astronaut the next time I applied.

I could not believe I rejected NASA's offer for a job! I had weighed the pros and cons heavily before coming to my decision. I tried to figure out if I had made the right choice while I drove home from work later that night. I asked myself again and again, "Am I making the right decision? Will they think I'm someone who is not serious about becoming an astronaut?" I resolved that I would continue believing that one day I would be selected to fly into space.

In the meantime, all I could do was keep my eyes on the stars because they never abandoned me. Life went on no matter what. When I came to a stop at a red light, or *luz roja*, I noticed the gold Lawrence Livermore pin on the lapel of my jacket. The light from the street-corner lamp made it shine brightly. "There is more than one star and goal in life," I murmured under my breath.

A little over a year after the birth of Vanessa, Adela announced that our fourth and final planned child was on its way. The sonogram once again indicated that it would be a baby girl.

Because of what happened with Vanessa, I took this news with a degree of skepticism. I was neither away on travel nor busy doing appraisals during the birth of our fourth child, so I was able to be present during the birth. This was a good thing since Adela had already threatened me if I did not show up at the hospital when she was in labor this time!

When a healthy baby girl was born on June 3, 1999, I thought: *Wow! Poor Julio and I are outnumbered!* Adela picked out the name Yesenia Marisol. I really liked the name and did not suggest others from which my wife and I could choose. This was apparently a good decision, since my daughter seems to have grown up liking both names; she now goes by Yesenia (or Yesi, for short) at home and Marisol at school.

Later that year, the Society of Mexican American Engineers and Scientists (MAES) awarded me the *Medalla de Oro* for my work and contributions to my community. Each year, thousands of engineers and students from all over the country gather at an event organized by MAES to talk about their experiences and share their findings. This event culminates with a gala dinner, where I received my *premio*, or award.

"José M. Hernández is one of the most prestigious engineers in the state of California. Our communities have benefited tremendously from his work on the invention of the first full-field digital mammography system for the earlier detection of breast cancer, which has saved the lives of many women. That is why it is with great pleasure that we award him the gold medal, our society's highest level of recognition."

The applause from the crowd elevated my mood to the point where I was somewhat emotional. It was a special moment for me. My hard work was being rewarded, and I could not have been any prouder to be an engineer. During that time, I was president of the local chapter of MAES. Three years after being honored, I was elected national president.

When the gold medal was put around my neck, I could see that Adelita was very proud of me. It was an honor for her too.

"I'm his wife," she would say to people around her.

"Pepe, you have achieved yet another milestone. How does it feel?"

"Oh honey, you sound like a reporter," I told her jokingly as I drove.

"Very funny. But seriously, how do you feel?"

"I feel very blessed and fortunate. But in all honesty, I can't believe it."

"Don't you stop now, Pepe. Remember your *real* dream. You promised me you wouldn't give up on it," she said seriously.

"I know. Don't worry. I won't," I said to her. She put her head on my shoulder as I continued to drive, and fell asleep soon after.

# CHAPTER 7

# Happy New Millennium

*And, when you want something, all the universe conspires in helping you to achieve it.*

PAULO COELHO (1947–)
BRAZILIAN LYRICIST AND NOVELIST

The initial countdown to the New Year, and new millennium, brought thoughts of what could happen in the year to come. On New Year's Eve, my family and I carried on the popular Mexican tradition of eating twelve grapes, or *uvas*—one for each month—and made a wish with each grape. Every time I ate one, my wish centered on one thing and one thing only: to become an astronaut for NASA.

I was still living in Washington when NASA began accepting applications for the next class of astronauts. I, as part of my annual ritual since 1992, once again renewed my application. By now I felt I could fill it out with my eyes closed. Although this was my eighth year of undergoing the application process, I was comforted by the knowledge that the individual who perseveres is the one who accomplishes what he or she has set out to do. Once again, I went through the selection process that I knew like the back of my hand: 4,000-plus applicants...down-selected to 300 applicants...and finally, the lucky remaining 100 applicants are invited to spend the week at Johnson Space Center in Houston, Texas.

For the second time, I was one of the 100 finalists. Just like before, these lucky 100 were invited in groups of 20 to spend the week and go through a series of medical and psychological exams, interviews, and tours of the various training facilities. Once all five groups were interviewed, the all-too-familiar waiting game that would seemingly last for months would commence. A mailing list of nearly all 100 interviewees would once again be created in which rumors about astronaut class selection were posted and fueled by mere speculation. While some on the list were second-time interviewees like me, others were third- and even fourth-time interviewees. Just like my first interview in 1998, I found myself in the subgroup that had its medical exams cleared and who received a security background check.

With the memory of having come so close but ending up disappointed as I did in 1998, I mentally prepared myself for the worst. On the other hand, I never lost sight of the prize and waited anxiously for the call that would tell me whether or not I was accepted.

When NASA decides to let the 100 individuals know whether they have been selected or not, the calls to all 100 people occur within a span of a few hours. It was rumored that if a candidate picked up the phone and the Johnson Space Center Director—who was George Abbey at the time—was on the other end, it would be good news. However, if it was the astronaut selection manager, Duane Ross, or any other interview panel member, one could almost guarantee it would be a "thanks but try again" type of call.

True to the rumor, when I received the call from Duane, it was to tell me that I had been seriously considered, but it was not my year. He then went on to suggest that I again consider an engineering position at Johnson Space Center. He suggested that although this would not guarantee another interview during the next selection cycle, it could go a long way in helping me gain the operations experience the selection panel noted I was lacking. He also told me that my current salary was somewhat high and that accepting such a job at Johnson Space Center would most likely involve a pay cut. I am not going to deny that I was devastated. I wanted to be an astronaut. I was already an engineer, and people acknowledged me as a successful engineer.

The idea of settling for something that I did not want to do was not an option for me. I had a good life, a happy family, and a secure job. There were moments when I thought I was obsessing a bit too much over a silly childhood dream. Chasing after this dream would cause me to once again uproot my family and, worse yet, take a pay cut. This was the point where I was convinced that I had to draw the line because I did not want the pursuit of my dream to adversely affect my family.

Even so, I believed that with a lot of hard work it was still an attainable goal. When I thought about how close I was placing in the selection process, uncontrollable emotion would rush through my entire body and keep me from concentrating on anything else. I opened my bedroom window that night to look up at the sky, as I did many times as a child. This time, I did not look at the stars. This time, I prayed.

*"God, you of all people know what I feel, who I am, and what I want. If it's my destiny to be an astronaut, help me achieve it. And if it's not, help me realize it now so I can go on with my life. You have given me a lot in life, for all of which I am grateful. But, is it bad of me to ask for more? I want to be an astronaut. Should I accept the engineering position? Help me figure out what I should do, please."*

Just then, a shooting star darted across the night sky the second I opened my eyes. As I saw the shooting star disappear in the night sky, reality set in and I realized that I had known the answer to my dilemma all along. I knew exactly what I had to do, or so I thought...

"May I talk to you for a moment?" I asked Adelita, who was watching television in the living room, or *sala*.

"Of course. Something wrong?"

"I want to talk to you about something really important. I have thought about the whole situation with NASA, a lot. But before we finalize our decision, I want to confirm something with you. We are getting ready to head back to California, and I'm probably going to get a promotion and a nice raise when I report back to work at the laboratory. That said, I think it is best for me to turn down the job offer with NASA. Houston is hot and muggy anyway; we'll have less money to spend and—"

Adelita interrupted me to say, "Honey, if moving to Houston and working for NASA as an engineer is what it will take for you to make your dream come true, then we'll move to Houston in a heartbeat."

"Are you sure? The salary they'll pay me will be less than what I make now. We're going to have to cut down on our expenses."

"Well then, we'll cut down. You know the old saying in Spanish: *Donde come uno, come dos*. Where one eats, two can eat," she said with a reassuring tone. "Besides, you should not give up and disqualify yourself because it's clear that if you don't accept the job, they will never select you. You are always going to have the *gusanito*, or worm of curiosity, inside your stomach, wondering 'what if?' Don't do this to yourself. Let's just go to Houston. If it does not work out, at least you did everything in your power to try and be selected."

Today, as I reflect upon this conversation, I cannot help but think how lucky I was to have married such a wonderful and understanding woman. Once again, she made *my* dream and aspiration *her* dream and aspiration.

I called NASA the next day to notify them that I had decided to go ahead and accept their offer. "I will gladly accept the engineering position," I told them. That simple sentence changed the trajectory of my life, as well as the lives of my family. I found myself having to move to a new city and state to start over from the ground up in order to prove my technical competence and worthiness of being considered for the next class of astronauts.

Convincing my family was one thing, but convincing my current boss, or *jefe*, at Lawrence Livermore National Laboratory (LLNL) was another. I called my division leader, Joe Galkowski, to inform him about my decision to quit my job with the Department of Energy and Lawrence Livermore National Laboratory. Surprisingly, he refused to accept my resignation.

"José, you've done an outstanding job these last fourteen years working here at LLNL and have consistently received outstanding reviews. If you don't mind, we prefer to put you on leave without pay. This will allow us to keep your security clearance active for as long as we can, and we will always have a position here for you—if things don't work out with NASA, which I'm sure they will," said Joe. "We certainly wish you all the best, José. I have no doubt that you'll make a fine astronaut."

I was quite gratified with how my current employer viewed me. Moreover, I was also gratified to learn that a safety net existed in the event things did not work out for me at NASA.

In March 2001, I drove from Washington to Houston to begin a new chapter, or *etapa*, in my life as an engineer for the NASA-Johnson Space Center. I made the move without my wife and our children, whose ages ranged from two to seven. The reason was that it was the middle of the school year, and I did not want to pull my two oldest kids out of school in Potomac, Maryland. I hated leaving my family behind; not a day went by without me missing them more than I did the prior day. I also missed my friends and the routine I had grown accustomed to back in the Washington, D.C., area.

My new boss, Gail, was a very polite Japanese woman. "Welcome to NASA. I'm going to show you around. There are a total of thirty-five engineers that make up the Materials and Processes Group. We do everything from failure analysis to nondestructive testing to advanced materials studies, such as the production and testing of carbon nanotubes." The name alone was quite impressive.

Gail continued to show me around. She looked back toward a lady before uttering her next words. "The woman in that corner office is Irene Kaye. She is in charge of the whole engineering structures division. Don't allow yourself to be put off by her serious demeanor. I assure you, she's quite nice," said Gail, to make me feel more at ease.

I appreciated everything she did to try and make me feel less nervous. Everyone she introduced me to was friendly and welcoming. I was not treated like the new kid in school. I was respected for being an experienced and accomplished engineer, just like everyone else at NASA.

My afternoons and nights were spent working, since I did not have a family to go home to in the evenings. I often worked into the late-night hours without even knowing it. I did not like being home alone. Luckily, my responsibilities at NASA intrigued me, and I did not mind spending my time engaged in them. It was only a matter of time before my family was going to join me in Houston.

My days were consumed with working on systems in the laboratories and analyzing data reports. It got to the point that I stopped looking at the clock on the wall. When the other engineers left at the end of the day, I would stay behind to continue working, with only figures and numbers on whiteboards and computer screens to keep me company. Noticing that the corner office also stayed lit at night, I realized I was not the only one who worked relatively late each day. One particular evening, I thought it would be a good idea to go into Irene's office to formally introduce myself.

"Good evening, Irene. May I come in?"

"Yes."

"I just wanted to formally introduce myself and thank you for this opportunity. I have learned a lot these last couple of weeks and I hope I don't let you, or NASA, down."

She interrupted me almost immediately and said, "Let me clarify something for you, José. I did not choose for you to be part of my department. Someone else placed you under my supervision. Believe me when I say that you are as replaceable as we all are. So if you don't feel this is the right place for you, feel free to apply for another position in a different department at any time."

"Very well, thank you," I said, as I walked out of her office, astounded by her straightforwardness. I decided to not waste my time and energy trying to figure out the reasoning behind her comment. I decided to turn that awkward situation into something positive. I was going to show her that I would become very valuable to her organization.

When the month of June arrived, marking the end of the school year, I returned to Washington for Adela and the children. On the way to our new home in Houston, I turned to Adela and said, "Houston is not as bad as you think."

Although she and my children had to learn to adapt to their new surroundings, it was relatively easy as we were blessed to have chosen an area with excellent neighbors. To the right of our home was the residence of Scott and Glynnis Hartwig; they would remain our neighbors for as long as we would live in Houston. To this day, they are our dear friends. Their two children, Brian and Kelsey, immediately became good friends with my four kids—Julio, Karina, Vanessa, and Yesenia.

Life in Houston with my family was satisfying, both personally and professionally. Everything went according to plan. We were well into the fall, the kids were in school, and our new house was in order. Every day I was learning something new at work. I challenged myself and strived to be as detailed as possible in order to give our customers high-quality results. Soon this was noticed.

One morning, Gail and Irene gathered everyone for an unscheduled branch meeting. "Everyone!" said Irene. "Gail, your current branch chief, will be taking a rotation assignment within NASA for the next six months. José Hernández will take over her responsibilities until further notice. That is all. Thank you."

I could not believe the words that came out of her mouth. The thought of me taking over Gail's position was not even on my radar. I was in shock knowing that Irene could have chosen another senior member of the branch for that position but she selected me. This announcement was all the more shocking especially after recalling my first conversation with her in which she almost encouraged me to leave her division. It was a complete surprise but a great honor to be named the acting—and later permanent—branch chief for the materials and processes branch; this was a role I accepted and took seriously without knowing what would occur a little less than a year and a half later.

In the meantime, Adela and I had decided that four kids were enough for the Hernández household. However, things do not always work out the way one plans. One day, before I left for work, Adela was experiencing flulike symptoms. She kidded with me and indicated that she hoped she was not pregnant. I laughed nervously as I walked out the front door.

When I arrived home from work that evening, Adela sat me down on the living room sofa and announced that her home pregnancy test indicated we would once again be parents! I have to admit I was very surprised. I was more shocked by this news than when I had heard of the other four pregnancies. Perhaps what scared me was the fact that now we would be parents to five kids. I am the fourth of four kids, so having a fifth child was venturing into unknown territory for me. I felt somewhat overwhelmed by this. Adela, on the other hand, is the eleventh of eleven children, so having five kids did not faze her at all. This baby would be different, too, because it would be a Texan, whereas our other four children and I are all Californians. When it came time to have the sonogram, Adela and I opted not to find out the sex of the baby.

On January 21, 2003, we welcomed our fifth child and second baby boy into the world. Antonio Miguel was a healthy baby. Although I was in a great state of shock upon hearing that I would be a father to five children, I now look at my nine-year-old Antonio and cannot imagine the Hernández household without him. God blessed us with five beautiful children, and I thank Him every day for the wonderful kids He has given to us. I also thank Him for my beautiful wife, as she certainly has been the foundation of the Hernández household. On many occasions, she has had to play the role of both mother and father because of my many absences due to astronaut training activities.

A few days earlier, on January 16, 2003, at 9:39 a.m., the space shuttle *Columbia* took off for its scheduled mission with seven astronauts on board. Without anyone's knowledge, the left wing was damaged during the launch when debris—later determined to be a piece of foam insulation—broke off from the external tank and struck the shuttle. The debris caused damage to a wing leading edge panel that served as part of its thermal protection system (TPS). This material, made of a rigid carbon-carbon substrate, provides thermal protection to the shuttle's wing leading edge during reentry into Earth's atmosphere. These panels, along with the tiles, attached to the bottom of the fuselage and wings to form the major part of the shuttle's thermal protection system (TPS). The tiles, thousands in number, are made of a silica compound, varying in thickness and shape; though somewhat susceptible to impact damage, they are also extremely effective in protecting the shuttle during the reentry into the atmosphere. It goes without saying that any significant damage affecting the integrity of any part of the TPS can result in catastrophic consequences.

After review of the launch video, it was reported that the piece of debris—approximately 50 × 40 × 15 centimeters in size—dislodged from the external tank and possibly hit the left wing. Discussions were held as to what that meant with respect to possible damage to the space shuttle.

On January 31, the day before *Columbia* was to land, discussions on the debris issue were ongoing. Meetings at the highest level were being held within NASA, and everyone was working toward gaining a better understanding, given the limited data that was available. Different scenarios were theorized, including ones suggesting damage to the wing, but most were put aside in favor of more optimistic scenarios. I believe a member of the Columbia Accident Investigation Board (CAIB) put it best when she said that a "normalization of deviation" had occurred at NASA. In short, many believed that NASA had desensitized itself from anomalies, and thus allowed itself to be convinced that this particular debris incident was not a serious issue.

*Columbia* was scheduled to land back on Earth on February 1, 2003. At 7:15 a.m. CST, the Orbital Maneuvering System engines were turned on for a deorbit burn. This burn allows the atmosphere to capture the space shuttle *Columbia* and

thus begin its reentry to earth. Within minutes, the temperature sensor on the left wing's brakes began to show an increase
in temperature; it was the first serious indication that something was wrong. At 7:59 a.m. CST, the last words from the
space shuttle *Columbia* were transmitted: "Understood, ah,
bah..." Three minutes later, *Columbia* broke apart, raining a
field of debris across the northwest parts of Texas and Louisiana. I, along with the rest of the world, watched it unfold on
television. I wasted no time reporting to NASA.

An emergency meeting was called and members of my
team, along with other employees and department heads,
slowly began to arrive. We gathered in our meeting room to
discuss the incident and mourn the loss of the crew on board.
We owed it to the crewmembers and their families to find the
answers to the questions we all had. To do so, we needed to
clear our minds and begin an investigation from an objective
point of view. An announcement was soon made: "There will
be no more missions until we discover the exact or root cause
of the *Columbia* accident."

I was still in charge of the materials and processes branch at
the time, which meant that my group and I would be supply-
ing technical support to the team that would investigate the
accident. What exactly happened upon entering Earth's atmosphere? We had to find the missing pieces of the puzzle and
put them together. Some of my branch members, along with
hundreds of others, were assigned to retrieve what remained
from the debris field that stretched hundreds of miles across
Texas and into Louisiana.

The scene that awaited them was tragic and unbearable.
*Columbia* had been reduced to nothing but various-sized

pieces that did not tell us much more than what we already knew, or thought we knew. Every piece of debris gathered from the field was transferred to a hangar at the Kennedy Space Center in Florida in order to begin the reconstruction and thus find the root cause of the accident.

The Southwest Research Laboratory in San Antonio, Texas, specialized in testing high-speed projectiles. This laboratory joined the investigation and months later, together with NASA personnel, confirmed—via experiments—our hypothesis. The experiments showed that if a piece of insulation foam of similar size and speed as the foam seen in the launch video broke off from the external tank and hit the wing leading edge panel, it could indeed cause enough damage to affect the integrity and insulating properties of the panel. This damage, in the form of a sizable crack or hole, would allow heat to enter into the wing structure during the reentry phase of the shuttle. The wing structure, made up mostly of aluminum, would have experienced temperatures significantly higher than its melting point, thus initiating the catastrophic failure the whole world witnessed on February 1, 2003.

The CAIB soon issued its findings, along with many recommendations, to NASA. The report and recommendations were well received, though it took a while for us to return to flight status. The *Challenger* and *Columbia* incidents always remain on our minds. They remind us that spaceflight has not yet matured to the point that a space mission can be viewed as routine and without risks.

In the fall of 2003, the selection process for the next wave of hopeful astronauts opened. Once again, I turned in my updated application. The fact that I worked for NASA did not guarantee my acceptance, and they made sure I understood that when I first accepted the job at NASA in 2001. I knew that I was just like any other aspiring applicant.

Although I was anxious for the selection process to begin, I can honestly say I was content and at peace with where I was in life. If I was not selected to travel into space, I would accept that, since I was happy working at NASA. Working at NASA made me realize that spaceflight involves tens of thousands of people and that every single person is as important to the success of the mission as the seven crew members aboard a space shuttle. In essence, I was proud of the work the materials and processes branch was doing and content with my continued support of the human spaceflight program through the efforts of the branch. I was also very happy with my family; five kids, a Labrador retriever, and a guinea pig were enough to keep one from obsessing over a childhood dream of becoming an astronaut!

Nonetheless, the selection process began and the number of applicants narrowed down from 4,000...to 300... to 100. A recommendation panel of eighteen individuals— made up of NASA-Johnson Space Center senior managers and astronauts—asked me a myriad of questions during the interview phase. The interview was designed to help the recommendation panel assess whether the individual would be a suitable fit in the astronaut office and, more important, a suitable crewmate for a space mission. I sat in tranquility when a familiar face asked me one of the questions.

"Why do you want to be an astronaut?" said Franklin Chang Díaz. I could not believe he was asking me this while sitting in front of me! I felt he put everything into perspective for me because I knew his story, which was very similar to mine, and that gave me the reassurance I needed to continue.

Life had taken me in many directions, and on this day, before me was the man who inspired me to continue dreaming during my days in high school. I believed it to be a good omen to have the first Latino American astronaut on the interview panel. Nevertheless, just having the privilege to be in the same room as such an inspirational person was satisfying.

My answer to Franklin was short but succinct. I simply told him that my desire to become an astronaut originated in 1969 as a seven-year-old, when I watched the very first Apollo mission on our old black-and-white TV. This event, coupled with watching the *Star Trek* original TV series, fueled my desire to become an astronaut.

I further explained that though I was not obsessed with becoming an astronaut the desire never subsided, and I navigated through my education and career with the hope of getting selected. I pointed out that the worst that could happen during this journey would be that I would have a very successful career as a research engineer. Not a bad consolation prize, I quipped

When the whole interview process ended, I—along with the other ninty-nine aspiring individuals—had nothing to do but wait. About four months later, I received a telephone call while working in my office. Frankly, I was prepared for the response that I knew all too well. However, this particular call did not come from the center director or the astronaut selection manager, Duane Ross. It came from a senior manager, Colonel Bob Cabana, who was in charge of the Flight Crew Operations Directorate (FCOD) and who was an astronaut himself.

I knew that if the center director was calling, it was sure to be good news. When someone on the recommendation board like Bob was calling, I really did not know what to think. I was puzzled. He started the conversation with the usual salutations and then went on to ask if I thought I was replaceable as head of the materials and processes branch. My response was genuine when I told him that I thought everyone was replaceable and that all along, I had taken upon myself the responsibility to mentor and train folks to be ready to take my place.

"Good," he said. "How would you like to come work for the astronaut office?"

I quickly realized I had been accepted! My whole body went numb the second I heard *la buena noticia*, or the good news; I did not know how I was able to hold the telephone without dropping it. A nervous laugh escaped my lips but no words came out as I listened to Bob continue speaking.

"Now, José, you cannot tell anyone beyond your immediate family about this because it will be announced at a press conference on May 6 at NASA Headquarters in Washington, D.C.," warned the voice on the other end of the line.

I agreed, said good-bye, and hung up. I did not tell anyone anything. I still had hours before I could go home from work, and I could not think of anything else but telling my beautiful wife, Adelita. She had to be the first to hear the good news, followed by my kids, and then my parents.

The ten-minute drive home seemed to last an eternity.

"Adelita, Adelita! Guess what! Our opportunity has come! Finally! I got accepted! I'm going to be an astronaut!"

Laughter, hugs, and kisses soon followed.

"And now what, Pepe? You've reached your goal. What's next?"

"Everything. My dream has just begun."

"Are you going to go on a mission?"

"I'll have to wait until I graduate from the two-year training program; I'm only a candidate right now."

"And then what?"

"Then I'll be able to fly into space and see the stars up close. Woo-hoo!"

"You'll be able to see *your* stars, José," she said. We embraced each other under the warm sun, shaded by the tall pine trees that are sprinkled along the perimeter of our backyard.

A couple of months later, most of the new class reported for duty. We received the blue flight uniform to be used during our flight training. I finally had a symbol in my hands that signified that I was one step closer to becoming an astronaut. "One step closer," I repeated to myself as I stared at the uniform.

I started to unwrap the clear plastic bag that protected my uniform with the ferocity I used to unwrap my Christmas presents when I was younger. I could not wait to put it on. The name tag read "José M. Hernández," the American flag was stitched on the right shoulder, and the NASA meatball logo was stitched on the right side of the upper chest. My curious hands inspected each and every pocket. I put it on and quickly tried to familiarize myself with the various pockets and zippers, before I looked at myself in the mirror.

Suddenly, I felt someone staring at me; it was my youngest daughter, Yesenia Marisol, who was four years old at the time.

She looked at me with a concentrated curiosity, so meticulously that she tilted her head from side to side to get a better angle of me. I thought she was going to jump into my arms and tell me how happy she was that I was now an astronaut; however, family has an interesting way of keeping a person grounded. Instead, Yesenia raised one arm and pointed at me. Then out came the words that brought me back to Earth faster than any spacecraft could ever hope to do.

"*Papi*, you look like Papa Smurf," said Yesenia, as she stared at me seriously.

By this time, my wife and the other kids had walked in, so we all had a good laugh. From that moment on, the Hernández household has referred to my blue flight suit as the Smurf suit.

May 2004 rolled around, and soon it was time for the new class of astronauts to travel to Washington, D.C., where we would be officially introduced to the world as the nineteenth class of NASA astronauts. The press event would take place the day after the fifth of May, or *Cinco de Mayo*, which is an important celebration for Mexico. Contrary to popular belief, *Cinco de Mayo* is not Mexico's Independence Day. The day commemorates an important battle that occurred in Puebla between elite French forces and an outnumbered and ill-equipped Mexican army, which the Mexican forces surprisingly won. The actual Mexican Independence Day is September 16, but I suspect "*dieciséis de septiembre*" is much harder to pronounce and thus market than *Cinco de Mayo*; this is possibly why the latter is much more popular here in the United States.

When the new team of astronauts arrived in the Washington, D.C., area on May 5, I was quickly informed that I was an invited guest at a *Cinco de Mayo* celebration at the White House later that evening. I was also asked to please wear my Smurf suit. Upon being taken to the White House by the NASA headquarters staff, I found myself surrounded by politicians and celebrities, including Emilio Estefan.

During his speech honoring *Cinco de Mayo*, President George W. Bush introduced me to all his guests: "This is José Hernández. He is part of the new generation of astronauts for NASA. Congratulations, Commander, on being selected."

It was incredible! Never in my wildest dreams did I imagine I would one day be at the White House with the president! Though he got my rank incorrect—as I was a civilian and had no rank—he was the first to officially recognize me in public as an astronaut.

The festivities continued in the Rose Garden to the tunes of Banda el Recodo de Cruz Lizárraga and to the music of Marco Antonio Solis, or "*El Buki.*"

The next day, the NASA press conference took place. I still had to keep the big news a secret from almost everyone. At 11:00 a.m., my fellow astronauts and I were brought face-to-face with the press. We were all nervous and careful of our every step as we walked in a single-file line—just like my siblings and I had when entering the house after coming back from school. When the cameras and microphones were directed at us, I remember thinking to myself: *I'm an astronaut, not a famous movie star.* My palms were sweaty and there was nothing I could do about it. We were introduced one by one: Satcher, Cassidy, Arnold, Dutton, and Hernández.

*Hernández?* Some reporters, or *reporteros*, were quick to notice my Latino last name and soon began asking questions: *Are you of Spanish descent? Are you Mexican? How did you get to where you are today?* Then, they wanted to know everything: *Tell us your story. What was your childhood like? Why do you want to be an astronaut?* It seemed as though everyone in attendance had their eyes on me. They wanted to know who José Hernández was.

At the end of the *conferencia de prensa*, or press conference, I found myself drowning in a sea of reporters. For a moment, I thought I was the only one bombarded with questions, but I noticed that my colleagues were too. Even my wife, Adelita, who was a few feet away from me, was being approached by members of the press.

"After many years of failed attempts, your husband is finally going to be a NASA astronaut. How do you feel?" they asked.

"I'm very proud of him!" she responded.

"Tell the Mexican press what you are thinking right now?"

"That I'm very proud."

Afterward, she and I could not stop laughing at how the only thing she could answer when they asked her a question was that she was "very proud." I told her—jokingly—that I would recommend to NASA to provide media training for our spouses.

We returned home to Houston to begin our astronaut training. I had to learn and acquire many new skills that are fundamental for any astronaut. It seemed as if the next two years would be spent drinking from a fire hose!

Our first big training assignment involved traveling to the Naval Air Station in Pensacola, Florida. Once there, we spent six weeks going to ground school, being taught water-survival techniques, and learning how to copilot T-34C airplanes. Ground school involved not only learning basic principles of flight, but also putting those principles to work in high fidelity flight simulators.

Perhaps the most interesting activity during the six-week training program was the one where we went on the submersible device that simulated the fuselage of a helicopter; this device is affectionately known as the helo-dunker. During this activity, four of us at a time were asked to strap ourselves into seats via a five-point seat belt harness.

Once we were strapped in, the fuselage would be lowered into a pool that was about twelve feet deep. Right before it touched the bottom surface, the fuselage would rotate so as to put us in an upside-down position. All this was accomplished as we held our breath!

Once upside down and settled in the bottom position, we were allowed to unstrap our seat belts to exit the cabin and ascend to the surface so we could finally breath. Safety divers were in position at the bottom of the pool in the event that any of us got into trouble.

We were asked to go through the helo-dunker three times. The first time, we could use any of the four exits; the second time, we were asked to go out a certain exit so as to crisscross ourselves. This was clearly an exercise designed to show that we could work together under stressful conditions. The third and final time, we were told that we could get out through any exit. The catch was that we had to wear goggles that were painted black, so we had to feel our way out of the cabin. All of this was done in full flight gear, including a flight helmet, harness, and boots.

When the water-survival training was completed, we were ready to start the flight training. The T-34C airplanes operate solely on a single-turbo turbine with one propeller. I already knew how to pilot a small airplane, but this activity was clearly designed for all of us to learn a new set of crew resource management aviation skills, utilizing different and more complex aircraft. Everything seemed to go much faster on a T-34C when compared to the small Cessna 152 plane with which I was familiar!

Once we finished the T-34C flight training, we traveled back to Houston for another eight weeks. Once there, we learned to fly an even faster and more complex aircraft: the T-38 jet trainer. This jet has two turbines. Under the right conditions, it has the ability to break the sound barrier. I thought back to the time I flew the Cessna on my own over Tracy, California, and how serene it was for me to fly at five thousand feet above the San Joaquin Valley while dodging the low-lying clouds. The T-38 was a lot different. Though the same complex controls were located in both the front and backseats, we, as mission specialists, were not being trained to be the pilot in command but rather a backseater. The backseater serves the function of a flight engineer while backing up all of the front seater's actions.

As we were training on the T-38 jet flights, we were gradually introduced to the space shuttle training. This training included academic courses in which experts explained, in detail, the fundamentals of a space shuttle's propulsion, hydraulic, mechanical, electrical, computer, aero surface, navigation, and computer systems—to name a few. First, we had to perfectly understand the systems in the classroom; then, we would be allowed to demonstrate our knowledge in the simulators. System failures were first simulated in a single system trainer so we could learn how to respond to various emergencies. Soon we were training on the multisystem trainers and responding to multisystem failures. We often did this in groups of two, as one of us performed the duties of the commander, while the other performed the role of a pilot.

Once we successfully demonstrated a mastery of multisystem failures, crews of four moved on to the fixed-based and motion-based simulators, which were high-fidelity trainers. These trainers tested our resolve in finding solutions to failure upon failure that occurred as we did numerous ascent, on-orbit, deorbit, and landing simulations.

Everything culminated with a certification run that allowed us to become part of the pool of astronauts who trained on a regular basis on these simulators. The regular generic training simulations we did served both to keep us fresh—with respect to our systems knowledge and operation of the space shuttle—and, equally important, to keep the folks that staffed the Mission Control Center (MCC) certified and proficient.

Once our two years of training and testing were over, we held a small graduation ceremony at Space Center Houston. Kent Rommel, the chief of the astronaut office, said a few words before presenting each of us with a silver pin with the astronaut logo on it. This is a symbol used for astronauts who have yet to travel into space. A gold pin symbolizes that an astronaut has already flown on a mission.

All my loved ones were there for me on my special day— my parents, wife, children, and close family members. They shared my dream; they were part of my history. I could see my parents beaming with pride, or *orgullo*! I was one step closer to my ultimate goal of going into space as a NASA astronaut.

Despite the celebration, I knew that to be named an astronaut did not mean that things would get easier. On the contrary, to be chosen meant that it was the start of a long, difficult road.

"What are you going to do now, *Papá*?" asked my son Julio, who was eleven years old at the time.

"Well, I don't know at the moment, *hijo*. Surely they will inform me on Monday," I answered.

"Are you going to go into space now?"

"Well, not now, but soon, I hope."

"What are you going to do in the meantime until you do?" he inquired.

"I don't know. I'm sure they will give me a ground job until it is my turn to go to space." And sure enough, the answer to his question arrived on the following Monday morning.

I learned that when an astronaut is not assigned to a mission, he or she spends 20 percent of his or her time in simulations and trainings, and the other 80 percent on technical assignments. My technical assignment for the next twenty-four months was to work as one of four astronaut support personnel (ASP) or "Cape Crusaders." A Cape Crusader's responsibility is to configure and make the final preparations of the shuttle's flight and middeck right before its scheduled mission. This job entailed extensive travel to Kennedy Space Center, hence the name Cape Crusader. We had to check flight systems in addition to performing vital tests and tasks, such as communication activation, to confirm that all systems were functioning and ready for use. We were also responsible for getting the flight cabin ready one day prior to takeoff. One of us served as part of the closeout crew that strapped the astronaut crew in for launch.

Though I was a Cape Crusader for seven consecutive missions, I most distinctively remember the mission where I was the lead, or prime, astronaut support personnel. That week, we worked diligently up until the launch time to prep the shuttle's flight deck and middeck. As prime ASP, it was my turn to serve as part of the closeout crew of six individuals. Members of the closeout crew wear white overalls with a number—which designates the specific duties of that individual—stamped on the back. For example, the number 2 identifies the prime ASP.

One of my main duties as part of the closeout crew was to help the suit technician strap the crew into their seats as they ingress the shuttle one by one. I was also tasked with helping them perform a communications check with the Launch Control Center (LCC) at the Kennedy Space Center and with Mission Control Center in Houston. While I did this, the other ASPs would join the immediate family members of the crew on the roof of the LCC complex. It was exciting to strap the crew in for launch, as we had a predetermined amount of time for this activity and avoiding delays was of utmost importance.

Once we strapped in the crew and the hatch was securely closed, we quickly dismantled the White Room that was used to ingress the shuttle and that served as a staging area for prepping the shuttle's middeck and flight deck. The White Room, located at the 192-foot level, was suspended via a walkway from the launch tower that came up right next to the shuttle's hatch entrance. Once the shuttle successfully launched, we hopped on our T-38 jets and flew across the Gulf back into Houston.

I remember this specific launch as being an early-morning flight. This meant that the closeout crew arrived at the launchpad at about three in the morning. We worked a couple of hours before the astronaut crew arrived and then, one by one, we started strapping in the crew. We worked in parallel as one crewmember from the flight deck, the first being the commander, would ingress along with another from the middeck. We would continue this pattern until we successfully strapped the entire crew in before closing the hatch and completing our cabin leak checks.

Next, we quickly picked up our equipment, dismantled the White Room, descended the launchpad, and departed to our assigned positions. We would then have a quick debrief. At approximately one hour after our launch, we would hop on our T-38 jets and return to Ellington Field in Houston.

On this particular day, I arrived shortly after noon. Instead of going straight to the office, I decided to get a bite to eat at my wife's restaurant. My wife, Adela, had just opened up a restaurant in Houston, down the street from Johnson Space Center, on the corner of Saturn and Gemini in the Clear Lake area.

A few years earlier she shared her dream of opening up a Mexican restaurant. When she told me of this dream, I thought it only fair that I try to support her in the realization of it; I did this even if it meant having to bus the occasional table or lend a hand in washing the dishes. After all, she had put up with me all these years and followed me across the country as I was literally chasing after my dream. Hence, we embarked upon the journey of becoming members of the business community. I could see the excitement in her eyes as she was planning the menu and designing the build-out for the restaurant at the new shopping strip. She named the

In Maine during a
wilderness survival
training course.
Navigating the way
back to civilization.

In Wyoming during
the winter as part of
the National Outdoor
Leadership School
(NOLS) winter survival
training.

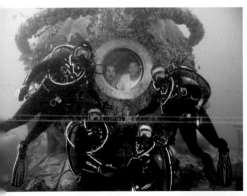

The NEEMO 12 crew before
beginning a twelve-day
lunar analog mission inside
of Aquarius, located sixty feet
below the ocean.

In the middle of a
six-hour simulated space
walk on the ocean floor.

The nineteenth class of astronauts getting ready for its first zero-G flight aboard the KC-135 NASA plane. The plane flies sixty parabolas where passengers experience twenty-five seconds of zero-G during every cycle.

José doing his best Superman impersonation during one of the zero-G cycles.

Stacked shuttle on the launchpad.

The STS-128 crew pauses during Terminal Countdown Demonstration Test (TCDT) activities to pose for a group photo. From left to right are Mission Specialist Danny Olivas, Pilot Kevin Ford, Mission Specialists Nicole Stott and Pat Forrester, Commander Frederick "CJ" Sturckow, and Mission Specialists José Hernández and Christer Fuglesang. The TCDT includes emergency exit training from the orbiter, opportunities to inspect their mission payloads in the orbiters payload bay, and simulated countdown exercises.

Arriving at Kennedy Space Center on T-38 jets and doing a fly-around the launch complex with Discovery on the launchpad.

STS-128 crew getting in the astro van on the way to the launchpad.

Courtesy of NASA

*Discovery* three seconds after launch.

*Discovery* in orbit during the rendezvous phase with the International Space Station (ISS) as seen by astronauts on the ISS.

Looking out the Russian side of the International Space Station with Earth in the background during a sunrise, which occurs every ninety minutes. Notice how thin and delicate the Earth's atmosphere seems to be.

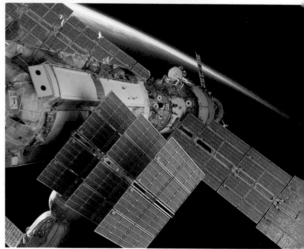

*Discovery*'s seven-member and ISS's six-member crews right after rendezvous. The thirteen-member crew officially represented five countries. Truly an international effort

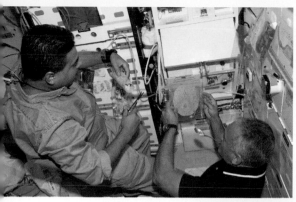

José and Danny preparing egg tacos for breakfast.

Typical day of floating in one of the ISS modules while performing various duties.

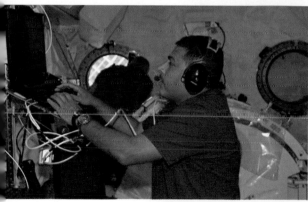

Calling home via the computer.

José in space, wearing a T-shirt of his alma mater, the University of the Pacific.

In orbit with the Mexican flag, later presented to President Felipe Calderón in Mexico.

Presenting a flown flag and the STS-128 patch to the president of Mexico, Felipe Calderón, in Los Pinos, which is Mexico's version of the White House.

Picture with the scapulars given to José by the Carmelita Descalzas nuns of Puebla. José later visited the nuns at their monastery and presented them with flown patch.

Looking out the window at the payload bay of *Discovery* while the robotic arm grapples the Multi Purpose Logistics Module (MPLM) Leonardo. The MPLM was about to be installed onto the ISS and contained more than seven tons of equipment, experiments, food, and water that would be transferred to the ISS.

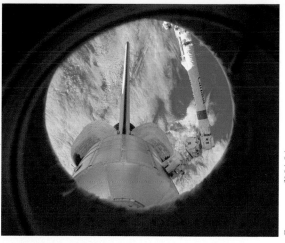

Parachute deployment after landing at Edwards Air Force Base.

After landing, the crew is greeted by the Edwards Air Force Base ground crew.

With President Obama at the 2010 White House Cinco de Mayo celebration.

2008 family Christmas portrait.

José with the student artists at the unveiling of the mural at Franklin High School, which is José's high school alma mater.

restaurant Tierra Luna Grill, which translates to Earth Moon Grill. Adelita had always prepared the best tasting *mole poblano*, *carnitas*, *chile relleno*, and fish tacos at home; now the community could also enjoy the fruits of her gastronomic talents. She was ecstatic that she would have the opportunity to share her authentic Mexican cooking with everyone.

That afternoon I arrived with two goals: One was to satisfy my yearning for chicken mole, and the second was to tell her about my great day strapping the crew in their seats and seeing the shuttle blast off into space. Just as I was halfway into telling her my story, she looked anxiously at her watch. She said that she hated to cut me off, but her dishwasher had called in sick that morning and she needed someone to fill in. She looked up at me in earnest and asked if I would mind filling in for him during the noon rush hour. I agreed, and unceremoniously fulfilled my duty as dishwasher.

I distinctly remember telling Adelita the irony of being married to her: At three in the morning, I was working inside the shuttle and I strapped in the crew of astronauts; then I observed the amazing launch. Next, I hopped on a T-38 jet and flew across the Gulf of Mexico. And now—of all possible things I could be doing—I was washing dishes at a restaurant! It goes to say that the family really does have a way of keeping one grounded. The restaurant was definitely an excellent tool both to rally the family around and to help Adela and me teach our kids the type of work ethic we had learned, growing up in migrant farmworking families.

In retrospect, I was happy with my accomplishments at that point. I was doing the things that I was passionate about in life, minus the dishwashing, of course. I was surrounded by a great family, friends, and an awesome work assignment. I also knew that my day—where I would be part of a crew that would fly into space—was coming.

Shortly after I graduated from the astronaut training program at NASA and not long after I began my job as a Cape Crusader, my alma mater, the University of the Pacific, presented me with an honorary doctorate degree at the 2006 graduation. It was an honor to have accepted such a prestigious award. I did so knowing that a distinguished alum, world-renowned jazz musician Dave Brubeck, was also receiving a special award. To my pleasant surprise, I was also informed that Clint Eastwood was going to be receiving the very same honor with me. Clint, though not a Pacific alum, was being honored for his work as the honorary chair of the newly established Dave Brubeck Institute at the University of the Pacific. Clint Eastwood and I would be receiving honorary doctorate degrees together. This was so exciting!

Finally, to make things even more interesting, I was informed that the faculty and the University Board of Regents had selected me to give the commencement address. Needless to say, I had some work to do in preparing what I hoped would be an inspirational address.

It is customary that the university regents and the special invited guests have dinner on campus at the university president's house the evening before commencement. During the dinner, I had the opportunity to meet outstanding individuals who cared about nothing more than the well-being of the University of the Pacific.

However, I must say that the highlight of the evening was when then-president of the university Don DeRosa asked us all to have a seat. There we were, sitting at a dinner table for eight: Don DeRosa and his lovely wife, Karen; Dave Brubeck with his lovely wife and fellow Pacific alum, Iola; Clint Eastwood with his lovely and young wife, Dina; and myself, along with my beautiful wife, Adela. Dina—who is of Puerto Rican descent—and my wife are roughly the same age, which plays into the next part of our dinner conversation.

Dr. DeRosa suggested, as an icebreaker, that we talk about how each couple met. Dave Brubeck and Iola talked about how they initially met at the University of the Pacific, which in those years was called the College of the Pacific.

I talked about how, at the insistence of my sister, Leticia, I met Adela on a blind date. I had just finished graduate school and was starting to enjoy life, while Adela had just gotten out of a bad relationship and was in no mood to get into another one. However, to pacify my persistent sister, we finally agreed on this blind date. On my initial call to her, we arranged for me to pick her up where she worked, which was the Adrien Arpel department at the Macy's store in my hometown of Stockton. Later I would kid around with Adela and tell her that the blind date was a low-risk proposition as I had planned to show up early; if what I saw did not please me, I would be a no-show. I, of course, had no such intentions since I already knew she was beautiful! Two years after our blind date, we were married and have been happy ever since.

The next story came from Clint. He talked about how he met Dina, a reporter, while she was covering a story in the San Francisco Bay Area. He asked her to an awards show, and thus began a serious relationship. Soon, marriage was on their minds and Dina, being of Latin descent, wanted Clint to ask her father for her hand in marriage. This presented an interesting situation because it turns out Clint is older than Dina's father! In any event, Clint talked about how he wanted to do the right thing and, above all else, make his soon-to-be bride happy. Next thing he knew, he was sitting on the living room sofa with Dina and her father. After a few awkward moments of silence, Clint finally gathered the nerve to ask Dina's father for her hand in marriage. The father, acting like a typical Latino *papá*, wanted to make sure that Clint really loved his daughter, and so he quizzed him on the subject.

After Clint delivered the "Why I love Dina" speech, the father said he had one more question. As Clint described it, they were there at the dinner table and the father said: "Clint, one last question, and please don't take this the wrong way, but aren't you worried about the age difference?" Clint, without skipping a beat, looked at his future father-in-law and said in his classic, raspy voice, "Well, sir, if she dies, she dies." It was at this point that Dina's father gave his blessing for the two to get married.

The next morning, as future honorary doctorate recipients, we were all dressed in black robes with gold detailing. Once again, I found myself standing in front of a mirror looking at myself. I was smiling the same smile I had seen many times before when I was younger. The only difference now was that I had a sprinkle of *canas*, or white hair, here and there. I was not as young in appearance anymore, but I was still young at heart. I still remembered the little boy who hoped a shooting star would fall in his neighborhood so he could find and keep it.

I could not believe that I was in the presence of actor and

director Clint Eastwood and world-renowned jazz musician Dave Brubeck. The music and procession began, and in walked a very famous actor along with an astronaut. When the event was over, Clint and I could now be referred to as doctors, and not only was a new title given to us but new friendships were made as we happily walked offstage. For the rest of my life, I would be honored to boast that I had received an honorary doctorate degree with Clint Eastwood!

A few months later, Donald DeRosa asked me to consider being part of the university's Board of Regents. The Board of Regents is tasked with the stewardship and financial health of the university. It was extremely prestigious to be asked to join this particular board. Upon showing my interest, I was interviewed and voted in by the Regents. I am glad to say that I am still part of the Board today.

Though Dr. DeRosa has retired, we have a dynamic new president who came to us from Texas Tech University, Dr. Pam Eibeck. Dr. Eibeck instantly won praise for kicking off the Beyond the Gates initiative. This initiative was designed to actively perform outreach efforts within our immediate community with the goal of increasing the number of students enrolling in the university from the Stockton area.

Everything seemed to be going according to how I ideally imagined it would when I was a kid working in the ruts and groves of the fields. Though my life seemed in order, there was a certain sense of emptiness. There was no reason for me to feel this way since I had everything that I ever wished for. Out of nowhere, I heard my mother's voice saying: *"What is the purpose of having goals in life, working hard for them, and achieving them, if you cannot share them with others?"*

Even though I was sharing this moment with my family and friends, I was still not completely enjoying my moment, or myself. This was particularly true after coming to Stockton to speak at a school. I felt the excitement my visit generated when I shared my experiences with elementary school children. But then, when I returned to Houston for training, it felt as if I had never visited Stockton. Something was missing, something that could give continuity to my visits. During this time, my friends and colleagues had called or e-mailed me to tell me what a positive impact my selection as an astronaut had made in the Stockton community. That was when the idea hit me! Why not start a foundation that capitalizes on my role as an astronaut and allows me to inspire kids to do well in school?

The idea of the *fundación*, or foundation, that would be called Reaching for the Stars was born. This, along with my work in helping develop the first full-field digital mammography system for the early detection of breast cancer, are what I consider my most personal and important projects; they have brought me the greatest satisfaction.

Angel Picon and Patty Tovar, two of my great friends, helped me start the legal framework for establishing a non-profit organization called the José Hernández Reaching for the Stars foundation. Angel and Patty put together a board and helped define the foundation's mission, which is to inspire kids to dream the impossible and to emphasize that, through education, anything is possible.

Presently, with the leadership of a retired Bank of Stockton executive, David Jimenez, we focus on encouraging children to become interested in science, technology, engineering, and math (STEM) fields. We are making new dreams a reality through scholarships, outreach efforts, a summer academy, and our annual hands-on Science Blast activities at both the San Joaquin Delta Community College and the University of the Pacific. This past year, I had the honor of addressing over 750 students at the foundation's annual Science Blast event!

I sincerely believe that from an educational perspective, much more needs to be done to help the next generation achieve even bigger things. If the United States is to remain competitive, then we must engage all segments of our community and afford them the opportunity to receive a high-quality college education.

A quote from Dr. Jill Biden, wife of Vice President Joe Biden, struck a chord with me. During a White House event where she was recognizing the efforts of community colleges, she said, "The countries that out-educate us today will out-compete us tomorrow." It was even more startling to read that the U.S. graduates approximately 50,000 engineers, while China graduates more than 400,000 engineers in one year! In short, we are already being out-educated, and that is why it is urgent to do something about this issue now.

I do not believe in just pointing out a problem and expecting the government to solve it on its own. I would like to think that this is the responsibility of every person in the United States and that the private sector and foundations, such as mine, should take some ownership for resolving this issue.

In short, foundations such as Reaching for the Stars need to work on increasing the level of interest of our children in the STEM fields so that these children will grow up and enter STEM-related careers. I firmly believe if each of us does our part, no matter how small, we will be in a much better situation than we are currently. "Whatever is planted will always grow," as my second grade teacher, Miss Young, would say when she talked to my parents.

I do not know how NASA chooses its astronauts for a specific mission. When NASA does make such a decision, they inform the selected astronauts before announcing the news to the rest of those astronauts' colleagues.

"You asked to see me, sir?" I said, as soon as I walked into Mr. Steve Lindsey's office. Mr. Lindsey was an active astronaut and the chief of the astronaut office. He was a very intelligent and slender all–American Air Force man whose grey-haired head stored a half a century's experience and knowledge.

"Yes, José. Please have a seat," he told me politely. "I've called you in to inform you that you have been selected to form part of the crew of the upcoming STS-128 mission. In about fifteen months, you will be at the International Space Station. We will announce the names of the rest of the crew-members at our all-hands meeting."

This was something that I had longed for and wished for my entire life! It was the preamble, or *preámbulo,* to my dream come true. My dream had been actualized. I found myself one step closer—a significant step closer—to flying into space. I thought: *Finally, my time has come!*

A couple of days later, we were invited to a conference room where I met my fellow crewmembers. I saw excitement in the eyes of everyone present. We were all thrilled to be a part of this opportunity of a lifetime.

Frederick "CJ" Sturckow, our commander, was the man responsible for putting the STS-128 training program together and assigning us specific mission duties. As he was an experienced commander who had traveled into space on three separate occasions, NASA trusted that he and Steve Lindsey had selected the appropriate crew for this specific mission.

The crew was comprised of the following individuals: Kevin A. Ford, the pilot; Patrick G. Forrester, the Mission Specialist 1; myself as Mission Specialist 2, also known as the flight engineer; John D. Olivas, Mission Specialist 3; Christer Fuglesang, Mission Specialist 4; and Nicole Stott, Mission Specialist 5, who would be part of a crew exchange to the International Space Station. Tim Kopra, who was already at the International Space Station, would then ride home with us.

"Getting to outer space is not easy. You have to be fully equipped and trained to be able to respond to whatever contingencies may arise. For the next fifteen months, you will be put through rigorous preparation," informed our boss, CJ.

I still can remember every single detail of our training. We learned to navigate high-fidelity spacecraft simulations identical to the one we would fly in. There were training sessions held underwater and exercises that taught us how to adapt to life outside Earth. In particular, one of the training activities was devised with the goal of bringing the crewmembers together as a single unit. We were all assigned one office from which we would complete our assigned tasks. In addition, we were told to pick one of three crew excursion destinations to go on as a team. Our choices were scaling the mountains of Wyoming, kayaking in Alaska, or sailing in Baja, California. We picked sailing in Baja, California, which we thought would be the most enriching experience.

The survival trip was intense, yet fun at the same time.

Rigging up the sailboat, preparing food, and learning from one another were all part of the process that would gel this crew into a tight and cohesive unit. We essentially learned to capitalize on people's strengths and, equally important, we learned one another's weaknesses.

After each tiring, full day of sailing, we would choose a site along the shore of the Baja peninsula and set up camp on a beach. Setting up camp was no easy task, as we had to tie up the boats and unload everything as we walked to shore in waist-deep water while trying to keep everything dry. Part of the team was in charge of cleaning the boats, while other team members set up the kitchen and prepared dinner.

The calm sea brought an inevitable silence that put us at ease before parting for our journey into space. I looked out at the rhythmic and lulling waves of the Sea of Cortez as the sun began to set, making me ponder: *At what point do the sea and the sky become one?*

The reflection of the sun's rays in the dark blue sea had me imagining the sunset over the dam of Ticuítaco, my parents' hometown, where I used to watch this magical event on a daily basis with my *abuelo*.

As the sky grew dark, my memory went back to the fields of the San Joaquin Valley where my first attraction to the stars occurred. I recalled anxiously wanting to get out of the car before a long day of work in the fields, still in the darkness of early dawn, to get a glimpse of the clear dark sky before the sun rose. My plan was to try and identify the Big Dipper, the Little Dipper, the North Star, and so forth. I enjoyed my moments with the night sky because soon the sun would beat down on me while I was performing backbreaking work, harvesting whatever was growing in the fields.

As a result of our sailing trip, my colleagues and I grew both personally and intellectually. We talked about our expectations and what our futures could hold after our mission. We also talked about our families, as well as our personal reasons and motivations for wanting to go into space. In summary, it was a great team-building experience where we learned to trust each other. This was something very necessary for meeting the challenges of space travel.

"It all started with believing in a dream that seemed unattainable and fighting for it against all odds. Seeing the light at the end of the tunnel when no one else would, or could, and suddenly realizing that it's attainable: This is what motivates one to fight even harder for it, without giving up. It's so close, you can almost reach out and grab it, but can't, because it's just a dream," exclaimed CJ in a moment of self-reflection.

It was then that I was able to summarize my *razón*, or reason, for them in my own way: "We are all astronauts and each one of us has our own star, the 'star of dreams,' as my grandfather used to say. Our life is the path to it."

# CHAPTER 8

# Harvesting the Dream

*All our dreams come true if we have the courage to pursue them.*

WALT DISNEY (1901–1966)
AMERICAN FILM PRODUCER, DIRECTOR, SCREENWRITER,
ANIMATOR, ENTREPRENEUR, AND PHILANTHROPIST

"Are you scared?"

"Not at all," I told my mother over the phone during my third day of quarantine at the Johnson Space Center in Houston.

"We're all praying for you, *mijo*. Don't forget that we love you very much."

As soon as her voice began to tremble, I knew the tears would inevitably follow.

"Your father and I will be at the launch with Adelita and the kids."

"I can't wait to see all of you there. Tell everyone I said hello, and that I'm fine. There's no need to worry. Everything is running smoothly."

"Very well, I will."

I immediately began to hear her soft cry.

"Why are you crying, *Mamá*?"

"I'm scared, *mijo*. And I'm happy and proud at the same time. This is your dream come true. I'm just scared something bad might happen."

"No, *Mamá*. Nothing is going to happen. I promise you,"

I said confidently. For a moment, it seemed like there was an exchange of roles: I was the parent who was calming a scared little girl.

"*Hijo…*"

"*¿Sí?*"

"Don't forget that I love you," she said.

"Never." A child can never forget a mother's love.

To think back on everything I had to do to get to where I was at that moment seemed like an eternal task. All my studying, preparation, and work were finally paying off. Just thinking about the individuals and situations that crossed my path in life made me realize how fortunate and blessed I was.

As the launch date approached, it became harder to *dormir*, or sleep. I tossed and turned for hours until I was finally able to sleep soundly. Part of the reason I was not able to sleep was because I kept thinking about what could possibly go wrong during the mission. *What if something fails? What will happen to my family? How will my wife, kids, and parents handle it?* Those thoughts disrupted my tranquility.

Luckily though, as the date approached, there was no time left to worry about anything but the mission. Our crew began adapting to a new schedule: going to bed at 8 a.m. and waking up at 4 p.m. We were forced to shift our sleep cycle because those were the hours we would be working at the International Space Station (ISS).

The closer we got to launch date, the more lucid our mission objectives became. Our first objective was to transport a new crewmember, Nicole Stott, to the ISS and return home with another astronaut, Tim Kopra, who had already spent more than two months in space.

Second, we had to conduct three space walks to replace one of the Station's ammonia-filled tanks, in addition to preparing and laying out all of the electrical and hydraulic plumbing needed to install the final module that was to be installed on a subsequent flight.

Last, we had to take an Italian-built portable laboratory called the Multi Purpose Logistics Module (MPLM), affectionately called Leonardo. The MPLM was one of three portable modules that can travel with the space shuttle in the payload bay. Once we docked to the ISS, we would attach the MPLM to the ISS with the ISS robotic arm. Leonardo carried more than seven tons of equipment, experiments, food, and water that needed to be transported to the ISS.

We also needed to bring back to Earth about a ton of equipment and waste no longer needed aboard the ISS. With all that said, we only had thirteen days to complete our three mission objectives. It was an intense and involved itinerary with no room for mistakes. I was eager to ensure that the mission was executed accordingly, and I know that my crewmates felt the same way.

During our rare moments of downtime, my colleagues and I talked about different things. We would say to one another with a smile, "We are a family." We even shared our personal stories of fear and uncertainty.

"Is it normal to be scared in the face of uncertainty? Even though it's my fourth time in space, I still feel like it's my first," said CJ, our commander.

During the space shuttle era, two tragedies have occurred in a span of over thirty years that have cast a dark cloud over NASA: *Challenger* and *Columbia*. Both incidents have been engraved in the minds of the American people. Human error is bound to occur at any given moment without warning. Perfection is only divine, and no one on Earth is perfect. "Only God, or *Dios*, is perfect," I reminded myself. We grow as individuals from mistakes and past experiences, which I did not realize until much later in life.

On March 25, 1979, a new generation of spacecraft was completed. A new model (*Columbia*) was introduced. If amortized over its intended use, the space shuttles were manufactured and intended to cost less than previous spacecrafts; they also had greater maneuverability and reusability capabilities, unlike spacecraft of the past such as those used in the Apollo missions. Whether the new model actually accomplished all of this depends on how the accounting is done. The space shuttle *Columbia* was launched into space for the first time on April 12, 1981, followed by *Challenger* a year later, and *Discovery* in November 1983. It was the start of a new era in low-Earth-orbit space operations.

The euphoria was soon shattered by the STS-51L *Challenger* disaster on January 28, 1986. It exploded seventy-three seconds after takeoff, killing the entire crew on board as a result of joint O-ring failure in the solid rocket booster. The seven crewmembers aboard did not get the opportunity to reach the heavens while still alive. Among them was a thirty-seven-year-old teacher, Christa McAuliffe, who was the first civilian to be chosen to travel into space out of more than ten thousand candidates who applied.

In 1992, *Endeavour* was introduced as a replacement for *Challenger*. The launches after *Challenger*, including those of *Endeavour*, were very successful. It all changed again in

February 2003 when *Columbia*, on its way home from a successful space journey, began to disintegrate in the skies above
Texas. Once again, all future launches were suspended until an
investigation board could report on the root cause of the accident and provide recommendations that would improve safety
operations of the shuttle fleet.

About four days before a launch, astronauts usually transfer themselves to the Kennedy Space Center using T-38 jets,
but for us unfavorable weather prevented this from taking
place. So, we were transferred on a NASA airplane that we had
previously used to practice our shuttle landings. The weather
was not ideal and that made me a bit pessimistic. It was not
like me to think negatively, especially during a special occasion, but this time I repeatedly found myself having negative
thoughts.

Our crew spent about a week in quarantine at the JSC and
KSC in order to avoid contracting any infections or illnesses.
My wife, Adelita, came to visit me periodically.

On the eve of our launch, prayers were said, blessings were
given, hugs were shared, and tears were shed before we said
our good-byes to our loved ones.

"Tomorrow will be a very special night," I told my wife
before we parted ways.

More hugs and kisses followed before our hands unlocked.

That evening, the air was calm and breezy. The sun was
setting, making my shadow fully disappear. Then, the night,
or *la noche*, was dark like Adelita's hair that blew in the wind
as she walked toward me. We were at the beach house next to
the Kennedy Space Center, where many astronauts have spent
time with their spouses before going into space; this is some-

thing that has been happening since the time of the Apollo missions. A pair of pearl earrings and a wedding ring further embellished the figure of the woman who always stood by me.

"Here I am," she said.

I could see and read many things in her eyes. We embraced and enjoyed a romantic candlelight *cena*.

"How do you feel?" she asked in her sweet, tender voice.

"Fine," I answered.

"The kids send their love. They cannot stop talking to all their friends about how their father is an astronaut."

"Really? Tell them I love them and that I'm always thinking about them."

"They know that."

"Look, Adelita," I said, as I started to talk about the personal items I was taking with me to space.

"I'm taking a scapular," I said as I described it. "A nun from Puebla in Mexico sent it to me when she found out I was going into space.

"I am also taking a small Mexican flag that I plan to present to President Calderón upon my return.

"And I am also taking a flag for the survivors of the World War II Mexican 201 Air Squadron. They are the only air squadron from Mexico who fought along with the U.S. during World War II. They asked me to please take it with me."

"What else are you taking?" she asked curiously.

"The crucifix that you gave me, our wedding bands, and five little medals of *la Virgen de Guadalupe*—one for each of our kids—as well as a photograph of our family," I said, as I pulled the wedding band from her finger to take with me.

Adelita could not hold back her tears and began to cry.

Thinking back, I do not recall a time I have ever seen her cry with such nostalgia and sentiment. When she got up to hug me, she clung to me as a child tightly squeezes their teddy bear, not wanting to let go. I could sense that she wanted to say something but did not. In my heart, I felt she wanted to say, *"I don't ever want to leave your side. I fear for you. You're going away, far away, and I don't know if you'll come back."* I could feel it in her arms as she embraced me. I could read it in her beautiful green eyes, which were fixed on me.

"Everything is going to be fine, I promise," I told her, as I caressed her face and ran my hands through her beautiful hair. I felt helpless that all I could do to assuage her fears was to hold her tight against me, not ever wanting to let go. The clock was ticking, and soon it would be time to part.

I had a serious case of insomnia the day before the mission. Even so, I was still able to perform the last-minute preparations that needed to be done before we departed. It had been a busy couple of days with barely enough time to rest, let alone catch my breath. The crew's to-do list grew so fast that we really did not have the time to realize that the following day was the one we had all been awaiting for a long time. As for me, this was the moment I had been waiting for since my childhood. The day before the launch, I told myself: *At this time tomorrow, I will be in space!*

We were ordered to rest before our big day, but that was nearly impossible for me to do. All my hopes, dreams, and fears were riding on what would take place the following day. The mind, or *la mente*, could not handle the countless thoughts rushing through it at the speed of light. It was not easy being an astronaut, and the workload that came with the title added an additional layer of responsibility and pressure. Nonetheless, my job had many rewards and advantages.

After years of yearning and dreaming, the moment of truth finally arrived. We had to wake up, or *despertar*, at least seven hours before our scheduled launch to prepare and organize everything. I woke up at 3:35 p.m. to realize that I still had more than seven hours until the moment of truth, but time flew (and soon I would, too).

Once we were up and about, it took a couple of hours of preparation in crew quarters before we, the seven astronauts, could head toward the launchpad. These preparations included listening to the weather briefings, having the suit technicians dress us in the orange launch and entry suits, and continuing the tradition of playing a game of cards. Steve Lindsey was waiting for us to carry out this particular ritual that began during the Apollo program.

"It's time," he told us enthusiastically. "How do you feel?"

"Fine," all seven of us answered in unison.

Steve was ready to play; he had a deck of cards, or *cartas*, in his hand. The head of the astronaut office—in this case, Steve Lindsey—was to play a game of high cards with each of the astronauts. As crewmembers, our goal was to beat Steve for good luck before boarding the shuttle.

Steve shared a few words of encouragement that were intended to ease our jitters. "Everything will be fine. Just do your best. Enjoy the experience and the spectacular view. Not everyone is lucky enough to have this opportunity. Good luck to all of you," he said. The stars seemed to have lined up in my favor. I was living my ultimate dream and nothing could stop me now.

I had been a part of numerous launches, so I knew the drill to perfection. Except this time, I was not helping prepare the astronauts for their launch; incredibly, I was the one wearing the orange suit, or *traje naranjado*. As I was slipping on the suit, countless childhood memories and photographs ran through my mind. My name was stitched on the name tag on the left side of my chest below a pair of white wings, which, as I liked to think, protected my heart.

We drove to the launchpad in the Astro van together, as a crew, smiling. *Discovery* awaited us. We were about to spend fourteen days in space, floating above Earth, underneath the stars.

We arrived at the launchpad and entered the elevator to go up to the 192-foot level, where we had access to the shuttle's hatch. A walkway allowed us to approach the White Room that was next to the hatch. It was in this White Room where we put on the last of our gear before entering the shuttle and getting strapped in by the closeout crew.

One by one, we were called in to take our seats. At the front was Frederick W. Sturckow, or CJ, as we called him. He had already been in space three times and everything was routine for him. Next to him was Kevin A. Ford, the pilot, who was about to experience everything for the first time, just like me. Patrick G. Forrester, Mission Specialist 1, was on his third trip into space. Then it was me: first-time flyer, Mission Specialist 2, and Flight Engineer. Next, in the middeck was John "Danny" Olivas, a fellow Mexican American whose grandparents were from Chihuahua; he was Mission Specialist 3, and this was his second mission. Swedish astronaut Christer Fuglesang was Mission Specialist 4. Like Danny, Fuglesang was on his second mission for NASA. Last but not least was Nicole Stott, Mission Specialist 5, who was also on her first trip, and she was the one who would stay behind on the International Space Station when the rest of us returned. Timothy Kopra, already on the ISS for more than two months, was scheduled to return from his first trip to space with us as our Mission Specialist 5.

Once on the launchpad, it took a few more hours before the countdown would tick down to zero and we would blast off into space. Members of the closeout crew exited the shuttle. The hatch was shut and closed. It was then that the closeout crew performed a cabin leak check and then disassembled the White Room to clear the launchpad.

During the last hour before launch, I sat strapped into my seat on the flight deck. A million different thoughts rushed through my mind:

- *50 minutes*: To keep my mind off the time that remained, I began to focus my attention on other things. I remembered my time spent in the fields as a child, harvesting different fruits and vegetables. I remembered looking up at the sky, dreaming about how one day I would reach the stars. It always amazed me how the sky in California and Michoacán was so blue.

- *40 minutes*: Mexico came to mind. I thought about how I would once again set foot on its soil upon my return. The only thing I wanted to do was breathe the fresh air where my grandparents once lived and walk alongside the dam in Ticuítaco as I used to with my grandfather. I also longed to go back to La Piedad to the kiosk in the middle of the town square where my parents met and fell in love. I thought about how pleasant it would be to drink a cup of coffee and sit outside the café in El Sorrento looking out at the town square.

- *30 minutes*: I was lost amid my own thoughts. I could not wait for the moment I would reunite with the entire *familia*. I wanted to hug all of them and thank them for teaching me valuable life lessons that helped me along the way.

- *20 minutes*: After all the hard work, sacrifice, and dedication that went into making my childhood dream come true, I still could not believe that my opportunity had come. I was thankful for all I had up to this point in my life. Who could have believed that a little boy from the fields of California with ripped shoes and old clothes would one day wear a NASA uniform? I was like the happiest kid that day, with sweaty hands and a heart beating as fast as when I first met my wife, Adelita. I continued thinking of the wonderful things this country has to offer to those who dare to dream; I learned that with a solid education, dreams can become a reality here in the United States. Just as my parents had promised me: *"Take a good look at one another,"* my father would say to my siblings and me at the end of each day's work in the fields. *"Is this the future you want for yourselves? You want your hands like this covered with mud? Well, this is what your future will look like if you don't obtain an education."* My dad was right. Having an education is crucial to being successful.

- *10 minutes*: *La magia*, or magic, is hard to discover, but I believe that passion in the heart and positive thinking in the mind are the two ingredients for achieving something extraordinary. Just ask a scientist, an inventor, or an artist—a simple idea or dream has given birth to some of our history's greatest inventions.

Suddenly, I heard the countdown reach the nine-minute hold. That is when the final systems checks are conducted by Launch Control Center (LCC). It was almost time…

"Make your final adjustments and prepare for takeoff," we heard.

"Cabin revision complete."

"Manuals ready."

Seconds before launch, the bottom of the launchpad was sprayed with water in an effort to cushion the noise and vibrations made as a result of the power dissipated by both the three shuttle main engines and the two solid rocket boosters.

Everything was going according to plan until Pete Nickolenko, the launch director, informed us that the weather conditions were "unfavorable." Fifty minutes later, our mission was aborted due to local thunderstorms in the Florida skies. The decision makers at the LCC, led by Pete, concurred that our flight rules prevented us from blasting into space that evening because of the severity of the weather. I put on a face that tried not to show disappointment, but deep inside my emotions mirrored the weather outside.

As we exited the shuttle, we looked at one another with disappointment. It was hard for me to control myself. I wanted us to launch so badly. I felt as if my dream was handed to me and then yanked away. It was unclear as to when we would resume the mission. Some of us thought a twenty-four-hour slip would be enough time to let the weather improve. We headed back to KSC crew quarters. We took off our orange launch and entry suits (LES). After cleaning up and dressing in street clothes, I consoled myself by saying, *"If I waited almost forty years for this moment, why not wait a few more hours or days?"*

A few hours later, a new date and time was announced for the STS-128 *Discovery* launch: Wednesday, August 26, 2009. This was a forty-eight-hour slip. The Mission Management Team (MMT), who had set the new launch date, obviously did not share our optimism about the weather improving within twenty-four hours.

That night, I slept on a regular bed here on Earth, instead of in the weightless sleeping bag I had been waiting to experience for such a long time. As the suit technicians hung my orange LES suit in the astronaut changing room at KSC crew quarters, all I could think of was putting it back on. The earliest that was to happen was on Wednesday. But as we woke up on Wednesday, we found out that it was not going to happen then, either.

"We discovered a defective fuel control valve, which is being replaced at the moment. We have pushed back the launch date, again, for 11:59:37 p.m. EDT on Friday, August 28, 2009," NASA informed us.

Once again, the moment of putting on my orange LES suit was postponed. To be honest, having to wait—again—was frustrating and annoying. Every time I looked at a calendar, or clock, it seemed like time purposely slowed down to taunt me.

We tried to make light of the situation and said that this only meant we were the prime crew for a longer period of time. Being the prime crew, which is defined as the next crew in line to launch, has its benefits. For example, the prime crew has priority in training and reserving T-38 jets to meet flight time training requirements. We would also say, *"Third time's a charm,"* to one another to boost our enthusiasm and morale. We knew perfectly well that if the mission was grounded once again, there was a good chance that *Discovery* would be grounded for a couple of months. In short, further delays would result not in how many days, but in how many months until takeoff. I told myself repeatedly that I needed to be patient. But how could I be patient when I was running on pure adrenaline?

On Friday, we once again found ourselves sitting inside *Discovery*, ready for takeoff. With only two and a half hours to go, I knew it was only a matter of time now before a button was pushed and we would be well on our way to space. The NASA team in Houston was confident that the third time *was* indeed the charm.

Suddenly, in the blink of an eye, the countdown clock was set into motion after having reached the nine minute hold. We could hear the countdown: "9 minutes...5 seconds...4... 3...2..." We closed our helmet visors as we heard the three main engines light up.

Shortly thereafter, we felt the gentle vibrations of the engines. About two seconds later, as the countdown reached zero, the noise level increased in magnitude and the vibrations grew more violent. The two solid motors attached to the side of the external tanks had ignited! Just as I thought the whole shuttle was going to shake apart or fall to one side, I felt a lot of pressure in my back. I heard "Zero...takeoff!" Through the corner of my eye, I could see the tower staying behind as we lifted off! We were on our way!

Immediately, the muscle memory of our training simulations took over. I quickly focused on my job as Mission Specialist 2, which was to execute the role of a flight engineer. I began reading off the predetermined milestones to our commander and pilot while monitoring the screens and gauges in front and above me to ensure none would deviate from their expected readings. The most dynamic parts of our mission were the blastoff and the subsequent eight-and-a-half-minute flight into space; during the latter, we went from resting on the launchpad to orbiting our planet at more than 17,500 miles an hour at an altitude of some 280 miles.

Two and a half minutes into our launch, the two Solid Rocket Boosters (SRBs) separated and fell to the ocean about 200 miles northeast of the Kennedy Space Center. The SRBs deployed a parachute that allowed them to gently fall into the ocean where two NASA boats awaited them. Once recovered, they could be refurbished and reused.

After the initial two and a half minutes, the next six minutes became a bit quieter and the ride became a lot smoother. When we reached eight minutes and thirty seconds into flight, we had reached the main engine cutoff, or MECO. This basically meant that we had reached our top speed of 17,500 miles per hour and had turned off our main engines.

The next step for us was to monitor the separation of the external tank, which was feeding our three main engines. The external tank typically ends up so high that it does not survive reentry into the atmosphere, and thus disintegrates into pieces before falling harmlessly back into the ocean. The shuttle usually possesses enough energy to continue upward and—when appropriate—begins orbiting the planet. Soon after this happened to us, we reached a microgravity environment and began floating in space, high above the Earth.

Our mission was well on its way.

## Day One

Time, or *el tiempo*, in space is very crucial, not only for NASA but also for astronauts. Each of us had a strict schedule of responsibilities and duties to follow. It was our job to keep on schedule to avoid any setbacks. The first thing we did was change out of our launch and entry suits and into regular, comfortable polo-style shirts and khaki pants. The purpose of the LES suit is to serve as a self-enclosed system that provides oxygen in the event of a sudden cabin depressurization during ascent or entry.

The second thing I did was to perform the installation of the portable onboard computers. One of the laptops gave us the ability to see which part of the world we were flying over via a NASA application called Worldmap. The photographs and data taken during our mission were also transmitted to NASA Mission Control Center in Houston via one of those laptops. The activation of the impact monitoring software also required its own computer. The last computer I installed allowed us to gain situational awareness as we approached and docked to the International Space Station. Tasks performed by other crew members included the opening of our payload bay doors, deployment of the Ku-band antenna, robotic arm activation, and payload bay survey.

It is estimated that about 20 percent of the crewmembers experience space adaptation sickness. I noticed it affected some of our crewmembers more than others. I admit to having a mild case of nausea during the first day, but it certainly did not hinder me in carrying out my duties.

I remember the doctor warning me during my last checkup, *"It's called space adaptation sickness. You will feel nausea like everyone else on board. It's an acute discomfort that will slowly disappear with some medicine in no time."*

My stomach did not stop turning, just like my *emociones*, or emotions. Luckily, the medicine helped me. Once we finished eating and hydrating ourselves, we each took a sleeping bag, tied it to the wall, turned off the lights, and went to sleep. "Good night," we said to one another.

When I looked out the small shuttle window, I saw total darkness, or *oscuridad*. As soon as I made myself comfortable in the sleeping bag, my eyes began to close on their own. Surprisingly, I did not think or dream about anything that night. The only thing I wanted to do was sleep. I had experienced and done so much work during my first few hours in space that I was really quite tired.

## Day Two

The second day of our mission was dedicated to the inspection of the thermal protection system located on the leading edge of the wings and the bottom base of the shuttle. To do so, three members of our crew took turns operating the robotic arm attached to the Orbiter Boom Sensor System (OBSS). Fortunately, after the inspection, everything seemed to be fine. We would have to wait until the engineers in Houston reviewed the video we recorded and transmitted down before they would officially declare that no damage to our thermal protection system occurred during our ascent into space. We also performed the Extravehicular Mobility Unit (EVU) space suit checkout, along with the installation of the centerline camera. The camera was important because it helped us dock to the International Space Station.

My final activity during our second day in space was to perform the rendezvous tool software checkout on one of the portable computers I had installed on the first day. The rest of the smaller tasks were performed according to our individual itineraries. As for my nausea, it had diminished, but not fully.

"Still not feeling well, José?" asked my commander, CJ.

"I'm afraid not," I told him.

"The other affected crewmembers no longer have nausea or feel dizzy," he said as he patted one of the affected crewmembers on the back. "Just give it some time."

"I hope you're right, CJ."

"It'll pass, you'll see," he told me in a semi-paternal voice.

True to his words, I soon began feeling a whole lot better. *Thank God!* Toward the end of the day, I got a few moments to sit back and enjoy the experience I was living.

*I did it! I am in space!* A subtle light amidst the total darkness shone outside the window. I saw my reflection in the window while looking out at the little, bright star. A minute or two went by before I turned my attention inside to take in my surroundings. I looked around and saw everyone *durmiendo*, or sleeping, so peacefully, but I could not. I was fascinated because the stars were so bright and they seemed much closer.

I could not believe it! I began to have flashbacks, thinking back to how I used to count the stars from my bedroom window at home. *One...two...three...* Every star looked different from afar, but here in space—though not much closer—each star somehow seemed more distinct.

## Day Three

We were about 183 meters away from the International Space Station. Our shuttle began the 360-degree rotation for the purpose of being photographed using high-resolution photography and video by the space station crew. The task was made possible using another procedure that allowed us to detect any damage to our thermal protection system. This was a new protocol in response to the *Columbia* tragedy.

"There are no reports of any problems," MCC-Houston informed our commander, CJ.

Next to the actual launch, the docking of the shuttle to the ISS was one of the most crucial phases of our flight. We approached the ISS and essentially did a controlled, slow collision into the ISS Harmony/Pressurized mating adapter-2. Our collision, or soft dock, allowed the docking mechanism to engage and maintain the physical connection by the shuttle to the ISS. Upon pressurizing the mating adapter and opening our respective hatches, we were able to enter the ISS. The United States and Russia took turns in assigning one of their respective crewmembers as the commander of the ISS. We were greeted by a Russian commander and his international crew of five. Once together in the ISS, we were thirteen astronauts representing five countries. *Truly an international effort,* I thought.

"Welcome to the International Space Station," said the ISS commander, Gennady Padalka.

"Thank you very much," responded our own commander, CJ Sturckow.

"We're going to give you our ISS safety briefing," he continued.

I noticed they were very happy to see us. I wanted to think it was because they liked us, but I kidded with one of the crewmembers and told them they were probably elated because they knew we were bringing them fresh fruit and vegetables. Most of them had been at the ISS more than three months, and it had been a while since they'd had an apple!

The ISS crew welcomed us, and they did their best to make us feel at home. Our *Discovery* crew was scheduled to spend nine days on board the International Space Station carrying out experiments and investigations utilizing the MPLM portable laboratory. In addition, we were to perform three EVAs, or space walks, that allowed us to make the final preparations for the installation of a new module on a subsequent mission. Finally, we were trading one of our crew members, Nicole Stott, for one of theirs, Tim Kopra.

## Day Four

"Is everything ready, José?"

"Everything is set and ready to go," I communicated to MCC-Houston.

"Very well then. Let's begin."

I adjusted the pan and tilt controls of the *cámaras*, or cameras, of the ISS and shuttle to give our pilot, Kevin, a clear picture of the location of the robotic arm as he maneuvered it to install the MPLM. The shuttle and ISS cameras were focused on the MPLM to ensure proper clearance and accurate placement onto the Earth-facing port of the ISS Harmony node. It was a slow and tedious task that required constant concentration.

Throughout all of this, I longed for a cup of coffee, as I was feeling the effects of caffeine withdrawal. We finally took a break and I was able to prepare myself a snack, including the much-needed coffee. Being in a microgravity environment, the coffee, of course, was not a typical cup because we had to prepare it in a bag and drink it with a straw.

As soon as we finished docking the MPLM, it was time for dinner. An astronaut's dinner is very peculiar. It is dehydrated and sealed airtight and requires the addition of hot water to be edible.

"We are having soup and steak for dinner tonight. And for dessert, we are having strawberries and cream," said our Mission Specialist 1, Pat Forrester.

"What about *tortillas*? I don't eat anything without *tortillas*!" I said jokingly.

"We know, José. You are a true Mexican," responded my commander.

It is not well known that *tortillas* are frequently consumed in space. *Tortillas* are actually a good substitute for bread; most important, they do not produce crumbs that can cause damage to the shuttle's equipment. I was so glad I was able to eat something familiar to my taste buds.

"Look everyone, José brought the Mexican flag," commented Nicole as she ate her strawberries and cream.

"I did," I said, somewhat hoping someone would volunteer to take a picture of me with the flag.

"May I ask why?"

"I wanted to have something from my parents' homeland. I haven't had the chance to visit Mexico lately, and quite frankly, I feel I have let go of my roots since the death of my grandparents."

"Something tells me that is about to change," she said jokingly.

Nicole was right. I had already received a call from Mexico's President Felipe Calderón to wish me good luck and to invite me to visit Mexico upon my return. It was my plan to personally hand him the flag I was holding.

The crew's mission continued. We spent our days working and planning for working. We also had small windows of opportunity in the evenings where we could listen to music, view our planet, and converse with other crewmembers on board the International Space Station. For the most part, however, there was work to be done from the hour we woke up to the hour we went to bed.

For some reason, I could not fall asleep on my fourth night in space. *What will happen when I return home from my mission?* I asked myself in silence. *Will things be different? If so, how?* Those thoughts were going through my mind as I got situated inside my sleeping bag. I felt as if I was floating on an imaginary fluffy cloud. I do not remember exactly what I dreamt about that night once I was finally able to fall asleep.

## Day Eight

> *It is my pride to have been born in the most humble*
>     *neighborhood*
> *Away from the bustle of a false society*
> *I do not have the disgrace of not being a son of the town*
> *I count myself among the people who do not have falsity*

The lyrics to José Alfredo Jiménez's "The Son of the Town" woke us up bright and early on the eighth day.

"It's mariachi music," I told them.

"Good choice," they said, smiling.

Each one of us had a turn to choose two songs to wake up to. For this particular morning, I chose "The Son of the Town." It is a song from my parents' era and I chose it in an effort to honor all of their hard work and their great sacrifice in giving their children an opportunity to obtain a good education.

> *My destiny is very simple, I want it how it comes*
> *Carrying a sadness or behind the illusion*
> *I walk through life very happy with my poverty*
> *Since I do not have money, I have a lot of heart*

I hummed along to the song while getting dressed and putting my sleeping bag away in its compartment. Two successful space walks, or Extra Vehicular Activities (EVAs), had been performed on two separate occasions. Danny was the only one scheduled to be part of all three EVAs. His first EVA was with Nicole; his second and third were with Christer Fuglesang, our Swedish astronaut. Three EVAs were required to complete the preparations on the exterior of the ISS.

The eighth day of the mission was a very special one for me.

"José, the interview is set up and ready. You have four minutes and thirty seconds to do it," I was told.

"Very well. Thank you."

I then heard a familiar voice.

"*Hola*, José! It's Carlos Loret."

"*Hola*, Carlos."

I was delighted to hear Carlos, a famous Mexican reporter, or *reportero*, who had been following my story for some time. Truth be told, I was terrified at the thought of knowing that millions of people in Latin America were going to see my interview. It was only after I returned and conversed with him that I found out he felt the same way. This was a historic interview, as it was the first live interview from space conducted in Spanish. The minutes went by so quickly that I felt my time was up just as I was getting started. We talked about the view of Mexico from space, including the attractive coast of the state of Quintana Roo on the Yucatán Peninsula.

We also spoke about my inability to detect borders that divide Earth into countries. "There are no borders from what I can see up here. Our world leaders should see how beautiful and precious our world looks from this perspective," I said to the reporter.

As soon as the interview ended, I headed to my next task. My next responsibility was to prepare for the third and final space walk to be conducted the next day. Danny and Christer were scheduled to lay and route the electrical and fluid cables necessary for the installation of the last ISS module to be adapted on the very next mission. Our crew spent more than six hours outside the ISS performing minor tasks.

While they performed their EVA, I was scheduled for duty at the MPLM. All day, I kept thinking about the lyrics to "The Son of the Town."

> *I compose my songs so the town will sing them to me*
> *And the day that the town fails me*
> *That will be the day I cry*

A few days later, my second song would wake us up. The second song I chose was one from my generation. It was Gloria Estefan's "Mi Tierra," which can be loosely translated as "My Planet." Without my knowing it, the song played on Gloria Estefan's birthday. Later that evening, our public affairs office forwarded me an e-mail Gloria had sent to NASA addressed to me. In the e-mail, she congratulated me and said she was proud I was in space representing the Hispanic community. She went on to state that she was humbled to know that her music not only played around the world, but also outside of it, in space. I was smiling that evening as a result of her e-mail. I was overwhelmed by how thoughtful it was for her to write me, especially since she did so on the very same day that the song woke us up! I was also pleasantly surprised that Perez Hilton's blog took notice of my song selection, saying something to the effect that for the first time, an astronaut actually chose a "cool song" as a wake-up song.

## Day Eleven

Our time in space was quickly coming to a conclusion. Pilot Kevin Ford and I took turns operating the robotic arm to demate the MPLM from the Earth-facing port of the Harmony module; the MPLM had to be installed back into *Discovery*'s cargo bay. We said our farewells to Nicole and the rest of the ISS crew, and we welcomed the newest addition to the *Discovery* team, Timothy Kopra. While some of the crewmembers where closing the hatch, I performed a check-out of the Rendezvous tools on the portable onboard computers. Once the hatches were closed, Discovery was ready to undock from the International Space Station and circle the space station before beginning its course back home.

## Day Twelve

Our first order of business was to initiate the undocking sequence of *Discovery* from the ISS. This activity utilizes a lot of crew resource management, and everyone was ready. Every crewmember had a job to perform during this phase of the flight.

Once *Discovery* was separated from the ISS by a safe distance, our pilot Kevin Ford would initiate a fly-around maneuver. Ford would have us circle the space station so that Tim Kopra and Danny Olivas could take photos and video of the ISS. This footage would allow engineers on the ground to review the high-resolution images and ensure the ISS had not sustained any structural damages as a result of micrometeorite or orbital debris hits.

Once Kevin completed the maneuver, we were ready to perform the late inspection of *Discovery*'s thermal protection system once again using the shuttle's robotic arm and the Orbiter Boom Sensor System (OBSS).

## Day Thirteen

This was the day before we were scheduled to return home. This necessitated doing some systems checks. We started putting the middeck and flight deck in a deorbit configuration. CJ and Kevin performed the Flight Control System (FCS) checkout, along with the Reaction Control System (RCS) hot fire test. The rest of us reconfigured the middeck and cabin stowage areas according to the landing configuration requirements.

## Day Fourteen

On this day, we made the final preparations necessary to begin the deorbit procedures. This included closing our Payload Bay Doors and once again putting on the orange LES suits for the entry phase of our flight. Once we were given the final all-systems-go, we would perform the deorbit burn; this would slow us enough to let the Earth's atmosphere capture us, thus beginning our descent.

However, the September weather at Kennedy Space Center was not cooperating. Precipitation and lightning were occurring within a twenty-mile radius of our KSC landing site. MCC-Houston delayed us one orbit. Upon a second orbit delay, we were notified that the weather was simply not going to cooperate that day and that they were going to delay our homecoming by twenty-four hours. Though anxious to be reunited with my family, I was glad we had an extra day. We were subsequently scheduled for some tasks, but we were not nearly as busy as we were on one of our regular days in space. This meant we had time to look out the window and observe our planet and the constellations while talking about our experiences and our mission, now that it was about to come to an end.

Observing the beauty of Earth from space was something I have not been able to put into words—well, not in a way where I have felt that I was truly doing the spectacular view justice. I felt goose bumps knowing that few people have had the privilege of looking at our planet from my perspective. I marveled at the blueness of the oceans and the whiteness of the clouds. At one point, I was able to make out the lights of some *ciudades*, or cities. *I can see San Francisco, Mexico City, and Houston*, I thought excitedly.

I managed to steal a few more moments for myself while the rest of the crew worked. Without anyone noticing, I made my way over to a corner, pulled out the crucifix that Adelita gave me, and said a prayer.

*"Let us, Lord, see your love in the world. Forgive us for our wrongdoings. Give us the faith to trust in your goodness. Forgive our ignorance and weakness. Give us the power to continue trusting wholeheartedly. And show us what we can do for peace on Earth. Amen."*

I asked God to bless my family, the crew, all the folks involved in the mission, and myself. That day I felt closer to Him than ever before.

## Day Fifteen

After spending an extra day in space, we found out that the weather at our primary landing site, the Kennedy Space Center, was still not cooperating. Hence, MCC-Houston called to inform us that we were going home that day, but we would be landing at our secondary landing site: Edwards Air Force Base in California. Though I was happy to be landing in my home state, I was a bit disappointed because it meant that our families would not be present to greet us. In fact, we would not see them until the following day, when we would return to Houston for our homecoming ceremony at the hangar in Ellington Field.

Nonetheless, the entire crew began making preparations for entering Earth's atmosphere. As a means to help with the adjustment from microgravity to the Earth's 1G gravity, each one of us had to follow a fluid load protocol. This protocol called for us to drink generous amounts of *líquidos*, or liquids, such as water and punch, along with salt pills that would help us retain water. We were allowed to skip the salt pills if we chose to drink chicken consomme before entering Earth's atmosphere. I opted for the punch and salt pills because I was not particularly fond of drinking cold chicken consomme.

"Prepare to turn on Auxiliary Power Units (APUs) for preparation to enter Earth's atmosphere," was the instruction given to Kevin by our commander, CJ. Finally, when we were somewhere over the Pacific Ocean, MCC-Houston gave CJ and Kevin the green light for the deorbit burn. That meant that in less than an hour, we would be landing at Edwards Air Force Base.

Houston remained in communication with us at all times. As each minute passed, the distance between our shuttle and Earth lessened. The planet also grew bigger in size before our very eyes, which meant that we were getting closer to home. In my mind, I was counting down the minutes, or *los minutos*, until we were safely on the ground.

Our landing point at the Edwards Air Force Base in California was a mere dot on our map. As *Discovery* darted across the sky at a high speed, I saw on our instruments that we broke the Mach 25 mark; at that point, we were traveling at slightly more than twenty-five times the speed of sound. I could feel the buffeting of the shuttle with the atmosphere, and I noticed an orange glow outside our windows. We were definitely in the atmosphere now; I noticed gravity slowly taking its effect as the weight of my helmet attached to my orange LES became heavier.

At about 26,000 feet, we broke through the cloud layer and had a good view of the ground both below and in front of us. By now, the shuttle had the characteristics of an airplane, as the aerodynamic surface controls were responding to the commander's input. The shuttle slowed down to normal airplane speeds and behaved more like a glider would, since it did not have an active propulsion system during the landing phase of the flight. This, of course, meant we had only one opportunity to land it.

Our commander and pilot had practiced these landings hundreds—if not thousands—of times in simulators and in actual approaches utilizing one of two planes that had been modified to be able to fly the shuttle's landing flight profile. At 400 feet, with the gear already armed, our pilot Kevin activated the gear-down command. This poised the wheels of the shuttle for contact with the surface of the pavement at Edwards Air Force Base in preparation for landing. The landing strip was ready in no time. Soon thereafter, we were literally racing down the landing strip until the parachute deployed and the pedal brakes slowly brought us to a complete stop.

We laughed and applauded the moment *Discovery* came to a complete stop. Our thumbs in the air signified an end to a successful mission. Everyone in Houston and at Kennedy Space Center in Florida began celebrating both our success and our safe return.

The opening of the shuttle doors reminded me of the times I had to open them to welcome back the returning astronauts. However, this time, I would be welcomed. And indeed we were!

"Welcome back," I was told by one of my class colleagues, Shane Kimbrough, as he unbuckled my seat belt.

We patted one another on the back once I was able to stand up. I exited the shuttle with a smile on my face. The seven of us crewmembers were beyond ecstatic. Everything went as planned. Our mission commander began to congratulate us and said, "We did it! I couldn't have asked for a better team!"

All of us had to spend an extra day on the base before we were able to go home. As I waited for the moment when I could go back to Houston, I could not fathom the irony of my dream of going into space both beginning in and concluding in the Golden State. As a boy, I dreamed of becoming an astronaut as I picked crops. As a man, I would exit a shuttle as an astronaut on a landing strip located just a few miles from where I grew up picking strawberries. It was poetic, really. There was truly this delightful symmetry to my life that helped me realize the importance of remaining humble and remembering where I came from.

When I examined the stark contrast between where I began and where I now stood, I was overwhelmed by what it took to travel that distance. While I was very proud of myself for resisting temptations to take a more pedestrian route through my life, I knew that my parents gave me the map that I used to help steer myself in the right direction. My family, my mentors, my friends, and my teachers helped me navigate through the roadblocks on the way to my success. My journey was just as much theirs, and I know that I would have never been able to rise to the occasion of achieving such stellar dreams if I did not have people who had helped to lift me up along the way.

I looked up at the heavens, thanking whatever forces of the universe came together to bless me with this life I was so happy to be living. I really had reached my stars. And now, I could think of nothing better than to share my accomplishments with the people I loved. I called my wife and parents—who were all in Florida—as soon as I had the chance.

"*Papá*, I'm back," I told him when I heard his voice.

"*Sí, mijo*, I know. I just saw it on the news. How do you feel?"

"Very happy! Why are you laughing?" I asked when I heard him chuckling.

"I was just thinking back to when you used to work in the fields with your ripped shoes and dirty clothes. You remember?"

"Of course I do."

"And look at you now—an astronaut who came back from space and you are okay!"

"It was you who helped me get to this point, *Papá*. Do you remember what you used to tell us every day after working in the fields? When we were all tired, sweaty, and sitting in the backseat of your car? You said, 'Take a look at yourself because this will be your future if you do not pursue an education.'"

"Yes, I remember," he said before silence ensued. "I could not be more proud of you, *mijo*. Look at you, from a humble *campesino* to an astronaut!"

My father's words moved me and made my voice tremble. I immediately called my wife, Adelita, after I hung up with my dad.

"Pepe, you should have seen all the important people who were at the launch. Everyone was cheering and applauding. We've seen you on TV, and people cannot stop talking about you guys. It's incredible!"

"And how did you feel?" I asked her.

"Nervous. I spent the whole time praying as the shuttle took off."

"I was praying too," I responded.

"I'm glad everything turned out fine," she said.

"Me too, Adelita. I cannot wait to see everybody," I told her.

"We cannot wait to see *you*."

"I'll be home tomorrow."

"Do you want me to cook you something special?"

"Yes! *Carnitas y mole poblano*," I said with my mouth already watering.

Personally, I do not know of a better place for *comida mexicana*, or Mexican food, in all of the Houston area than my wife's restaurant, Tierra Luna Grill. What I missed most when I was away from home were her specialty dishes. In space, the closest we came to her cooking was when Danny Olivas and I prepared breakfast burritos for the entire crew. Though they tasted good, they certainly did not measure up to her chorizo breakfast burritos. I also missed getting to roll up my sleeves, put on an apron, and wash some dishes at the restaurant on the weekends, which became a weekly task after my stint helping Adela the day her dishwasher called in sick. I knew I had to pitch in and help her because I had been married long enough to know that doing certain things with a smile on my face was necessary to preserve harmony in the household!

We were all able to go home the day after returning from space. My cell phone would not stop ringing; it was either a congratulatory message or an interview request. The number of voice mails I had was absurd. I knew I had plenty of time to listen to and respond to them, but the only thing I wanted to do was go home and sleep. Everything had happened so fast; I felt like there had been no time to process it all.

"*Papá! Papá!* You're back!" yelled *mis hijos*, or my children, as they rushed toward me.

I was exiting the NASA plane that transported the entire *Discovery* crew from California to Houston. Adelita was running behind them. Her glowing green eyes welcomed me, and I gazed into them as I kissed her.

I was bombarded with questions and I did not have time to answer a single one of them. It was difficult to make my way to the hangar where fellow NASA employees, as well as members of the press, were waiting. The bombardment of questions had not ceased for long before I found myself with microphones shoved in my face.

*"How do you feel?"*

*"What were you thinking as you launched into space?"*

*"Did you miss home?"*

*"Do you think you'll fly another mission?"*

*"How did you adapt to life in space?"*

My parents and my brother Gil were also waiting for me in the hangar.

*"Hijo!* You're back! My prayers have been answered," said my mother, as she clung to my arms.

"I did it, *Mamá*! I went into space!"

"Yes, you did. After years of dreaming about it and working hard for it, you finally did it! I'm so proud of you, *mijo*!"

"I cannot begin to thank you and *Papá* for all the sacrifices you made throughout the years," I told her, as I placed my hand on my father's back. "The two of you planted the seed from which this experience grew."

"And you harvested it," interjected my father with tears in his eyes.

I spent the whole afternoon, or *tarde*, at home with them. I turned off my phone so I could tell them about my adventure in space without interruptions. My wife and kids were silent and attentive while I spoke. I told them about how I slept in a floating sleeping bag, showered with a wet sponge, and prepared my dehydrated meals. In addition, I told them about how things floated around and how Earth looked from afar. I do not think I left out a single detail. At one point, I felt like I was telling them about a science fiction film I had seen.

"*Papá*, did you see God?" asked Karina.

"No, but he was right there with me."

"How do you know that?"

"Because I felt His presence."

Karina then looked at me with a *sonrisa*, or smile, that I had never seen before. It was as if my words confirmed to her that someone did hear her prayers when she kneeled down to talk to the Divine each night.

"So He does exist," she commented.

"Yes, Karina, He does."

"Are you now going to get a gold astronaut pin like the other astronauts wear?" asked my daughter Vanessa. She was referring to the gold pin in the shape of the astronaut logo that each astronaut receives in a ceremony after their first space-flight.

"Of course I will, and you will all be present when they pin it on me!" I told her.

"It's time for bed now," said Adelita, as she got up from the couch. "We'll continue this tomorrow. Your father has to rest now."

I made sure not to wake anyone when I got up in the middle of the night to go to the living room. Something triggered me to want to look at old photographs of myself throughout the years. Afterward, I went back to my room and I stood there in front of the mirror. *Am I really living this life?* I stepped back to look at myself from head to toe. The NASA STS-128 logo on my polo shirt, or *camiseta*, glared in the moonlight.

I went back to the living room and sat down on the couch. Newspaper clippings, letters of recognition, and photos with important individuals were scattered across my coffee table. The forty-seven years of my life were summarized in a pile of images and words. My life story stared me in the face.

One photograph in particular caught my attention. It was one in which I was holding a single tomato in one hand, and a bucket full of tomatoes in the other. I was wearing an old blue T-shirt and a pair of shoes that were ripped. My *abuelo* José and my siblings stood beside me. My *abuelo* posed with his straw hat. We were all wearing old, dirty clothes. The agricultural field seemed infinite in the background. The color of the shirt I was wearing in the photo was the exact color of the shirt I was wearing as I gazed at the picture at that moment. I had to smile, thinking about how things in life came full circle. I was now wearing a blue NASA polo shirt and not an old blue T-shirt.

I continued looking at many other old photographs from my childhood and adolescent years, along with pictures of my wedding and early days at NASA. As I did so, I thought about what the future could still have left for me. *Who will I meet? What will happen to me? What will I do?* Of course, it was impossible to know what was going to happen down the road, but just thinking about the different possibilities was exciting.

After checking in on my children while they were sleeping, a familiar sensation guided me outside to the backyard. The grass, or *el césped*, was wet with early-morning dew.

I had spent fourteen days in space; my dream had come true! I had seen the stars closer than most people on Earth ever had. I was blessed. It was as if those stars had waited for me my entire life so that I could meet them up close. Those stars witnessed the moment I was born, the moment I fell in love, and the moment I reached out to them. They are always watching, protecting, or calling me. From a distance, they are tiny sparkling lights of hope, but up close, they are what dreams are made of.

I thought of all the people who had crossed my path: friends, family, teachers, and coworkers. All of them were responsible for a small *parte*, or part, of my success in life. Each one of them believed a raggedy-dressed little boy from the fields could one day make his dream of traveling into space a reality. The difficult lives many of my childhood friends lived taught me that life is not always fair, and it is not always easy. A junior high school teacher taught me the beauty of my Mexican culture and homeland. The death of both a friend and a coworker's wife pushed me to help design a machine for the early detection of breast cancer. And my grandparents, who helped raise me, had loved me and nurtured me; never once did they allow me to forget how special I was.

"Make a wish, José," my grandfather would tell me whenever we saw a shooting star cross the night sky above Michoacán.

*"I wish to be an astronaut,"* I would say deep down in my heart.

It dawned on me that there is no secret formula or magic for making dreams come true. The only way to make a dream come true is to have the passion, the work ethic, and the foundation of a good education to help one go from one step to the next, while pushing aside the obstacles in life. *La educación*, or education, is crucial for whatever you do in life. It is fundamental when venturing out into the world.

I have a bachelor's degree, a master's degree, coursework

toward a PhD, and an extensive portfolio of research in the hard sciences; yet I still believe in God. I do not think I am alone in my belief that God answers prayers. I have lost count of the times He has sent me signs or made His presence known to me. *"Have no fear,"* is what I heard Him say to me when I was growing restless before going into space. It was the same answer, or *respuesta*, I got when I huddled in a corner of the shuttle to pray that nothing would go wrong during the mission.

A shiver ran through my entire body when I saw a shooting star as I gazed up at the sky. I took a second to make a wish. "I wish that my life does not pass in vain," I whispered.

I had the opportunity to experience and see unimaginable wonders when I was in space. My little existence is nothing compared to everything else in the universe. However, we are all living people, capable of doing great things for the sake of humanity, or *la humanidad*. With that said, I want to leave behind a legacy that will inspire others. We cannot go through life without aspirations or goals.

"I wish that my life does not pass in vain," I repeated. I want someone to hear, or read, about my story and feel the way I did when I learned about Franklin Chang-Diaz. I want a child to look up at the sky and say, "If he could do it, I can too!"

Nothing is impossible. If people would put aside their insecurities and believe in themselves, they would realize that everything is possible. *Todo es posible.* I remember what Adelita told me when I tossed my rejection letter from NASA on the floor: "If you are not going to be an astronaut, let it be because NASA says no, not because you gave up." Wise words of encouragement from someone you love and trust can make all the difference in your life.

*I wish that my life will not pass in vain.* I just want to be happy and healthy for the remainder of my life. I want to breathe fresh air and drink a cup of coffee back in the Central Valley of California. I want to be able to spend as much time as possible with my children—Julio, Karina, Vanessa, Yesenia, Antonio—and with my beautiful wife, Adelita. I want to have a deep and meaningful relationship with each of the rest of the members of my family. I want to leave behind my footprints for many people to follow in. I do this in the hope that perhaps my story may inspire others to leave behind a trail of their own footprints for a new generation to follow in. Only then can they reach their own stars and inspire others to do the same, creating a better world one idea or one dream at a time.

# Epilogue

Upon my return from space, a new chapter of my life unfolded. "What now?" I asked myself. And with that in mind, I decided to consider embarking on new adventures.

When I returned to the Johnson Space Center in Houston, I was asked to serve in NASA Headquarters' office in Washington, D.C., in the Office of Legislative and Intergovernmental Affairs (OLIA). I would be working to promote the president's agenda on space exploration and other space-related issues to Congress. I took the job with utmost pride.

And so I spent a year working on both the planning of and the budget allocation for future flight expeditions. My work was focused on helping continue to explore Earth and space from a short distance known as low Earth orbit—as it has been done for the past forty years—and moving on to longer-distance space exploration known as beyond low Earth orbit. The latter implies not only returning humans to the Moon, but also landing on and exploring asteroids, Mars, and the space beyond.

Part of the strategy to achieve these goals was to design a plan that would help the private sector develop low-Earth-orbit capabilities. This would not only allow the private sector to develop a "space tourism" industry, but it would also allow it to service the International Space Station (ISS)—including the transport of NASA astronauts to and from the ISS. If such a plan could be successfully implemented, this would allow

NASA to focus funding on beyond-low-Earth-orbit activities. Such endeavors would inevitably result in the development of new technologies in the areas of space propulsion, life-support systems, communications, radiation protection, and food growth. Technologies that allow for the adaptation or mitigation of the effects of long-duration spaceflights on bone density, muscular atrophy, and psychological health would likely result from NASA's new research. In turn, such technological advancements would undoubtedly have a significant effect on spin-off applications for use on Earth. This project was presented to the president, federal authorities, and senators, which left me with much satisfaction—professionally and personally.

After working at OLIA for a year, I returned to Houston to learn of the ongoing selection process of the next spaceflight crew. Due to the recent retirement of the space shuttle fleet, this crew and future crews would only be for long-duration missions to the International Space Station aboard a Russian Soyuz. This change meant that if I wanted to be part of the mission, I would have to train for two and a half years in the United States, Russia, Japan, Canada, and Europe. That alone would have forced me to be away from home about 80 percent of the time. In addition, my stay at the International Space Station would be for a minimum of six months.

Making drastic changes in my life was no longer something I could do while thinking only of myself and my desires, because my choices would also affect the lives of my wife and children. Choosing to go on a mission at that point in my life was a tough decision to make, and I faced many sleepless nights asking God for guidance. I ached to go back to space, excitedly imagining what my next journey into the final frontier could hold. Then I imagined what my days away from home would be like for my dear Adelita and how lonely she would feel. I thought of how important it was to me to see my children raised by both of their parents. Ultimately, I came to the conclusion that I would let the opportunity pass by because I could not afford—nor did I want—to be away from my family for three years. It was time for me to close a very important and meaningful chapter of my life. In January 2011, I retired from NASA.

It was not long before God sent the sign for which I had yearned. I was fortunate because my aerospace career did not end. A private business focused in the same field of work asked me to join their team. It filled me with joy. *I would have the best of both worlds*, I thought to myself. On one hand, I would be with my family; on the other hand, I would continue working in a field that fascinated me. I joined MEI Technologies, Inc., as their executive director of strategic operations.

My new position gave me the time to personally carry out an activity I greatly enjoy: sharing my experiences at conferences. I have traveled throughout the United States, Mexico, and the rest of Latin America to deliver speeches to students and workers. I have done so with the hope that my personal experience can inspire others to reach their own goals, no matter the constraints or limitations they believe may exist. I have visited numerous universities where I have come in close contact with students who eagerly listen to my story, all of them hoping to gain some insight as to how to move forward with their own. The students' applause, congratulations for my accomplishments, and reactions as I retell what my eyes witnessed from above are simply priceless. The main message of my speech—and really, of my life—is that *anything is possible*. I share with everyone the magical recipe for success that I applied to my own life. It is a recipe that I learned from my parents, and I also share it with you here:

1. Identify your goal in life.
2. Realize and understand how far you are away from that goal.
3. Develop a road map to get there. (Don't skip steps!)
4. Get yourself a good education consistent with your goal.
5. Develop a good work ethic and put your heart into reaching your goal.
6. Exemplify perseverance. Never give up on your dream, and remember that it is the journey—not the destination—that is of most importance.

These are not the steps to become an astronaut. These are the steps to harvest your own stars. The recipe works for anyone, in any part of the world, and trust me—it is infallible.

What came to your mind while in space? Did this experience change your view of life? Those are the two of the most common questions I get asked and I would like to share my responses with you.

As the countdown neared zero before takeoff, everything intensified: the noise, the power of the turbines, and even my own feelings. There were three hours before takeoff, which gave me more than enough time to look back at my life. I recalled the moments I spent working in the agricultural fields with my family, the images of the first man on the Moon, and all of the challenges I overcame to be there, sitting, buckled up in a space shuttle. It was exhilarating to live the moment I had been waiting for—the moment I had been working toward—for years.

When the moment for takeoff arrived, I felt pressure in my chest; it felt similar to having a newborn lie on my chest—a sensation I knew all too well, for I already had five children. As the shuttle elevated, it felt as if the imaginary baby's weight increased with my own weight. Shortly thereafter, it felt as if I was carrying the weight of two adults, and that made it difficult for me to breathe. Within eight minutes, we had already exited Earth's atmosphere. It was not long after that when we felt the effects of a microgravity environment, which caused us to float and feel extremely light in weight. Nevertheless, the seat belts kept us locked in place.

After being seated for more than an hour as I conducted my flight engineering tasks, I unbuckled my seat belt. The first thing I did, as I floated off my seat, was to propel myself forward. Doing my best Superman impersonation, I headed toward the middeck window to view the world from the unique perspective of space.

As I floated, memories of my childhood flashed through my mind. I thought back to my geography class in fourth grade when the teacher had a globe on her desk. "This is Spain. This is Portugal. Italy has the shape of a boot," the teacher would say. In my memory, I was able to distinguish the different countries from one another because they were demarcated by different colors on the map. I certainly did not expect to see such differences from space, but I thought I would be able to distinguish where one country ended and another one began. When I spotted the North American continent, I was able to find Canada. Surprisingly though, it was impossible to recognize where Canada ended and the United States began. I encountered the same problem when it came to distinguishing the borders between the United States and Mexico, and Central America and South America. I glanced out the window, looking closely until I found Central America.

I thought, *My gosh! I had to leave our planet to come to the conclusion that we are all one.* Borders are divisions that have been created by humans. *Wouldn't it be wonderful if our world leaders could live this same experience?* I thought. Perhaps they could see why we should all come together in times of need, why we should not discriminate against others on the basis of geography—or anything else, from a person's skin color to religion to gender. If other people were able to look at the world from the same perspective that I did, I am convinced that our planet would be a much better place.

During the span of our fourteen-day-long mission, I went around the Earth some 217 times. In other words, I traveled 5.7 million miles (9,173,260.8 kilometers). My wife, Adelita, would later joke with me about this, saying, "You have a lot of mileage." To which I would respond, "And with God's will, there may still be much more to go!" This being said, the distance we traveled meant that we orbited Earth every ninety minutes, so our days and nights each lasted approximately forty-five minutes. Explaining the timing element of our trip helps preface my second memorable moment in space, which came during my Earth observation activities.

During one of those night-day orbit cycles, the sunlight shone on the atmosphere at just the right angle so that I could see the thickness of the atmosphere delicately wrapped around the Earth. What I saw surprised me, as the atmosphere looked so thin and so delicate! It was impressive to realize that only this thin layer of protection is what is keeping us alive. This made me recognize the importance of our everyday actions here on Earth. Our environmentalists are correct in saying that everything we do today will be reflected in the lives of our children and our grandchildren. Looking down at the brilliant blue seas and the white, wispy clouds helped me come to the realization that it is so important to be a good steward of our planet and to do my part in helping to preserve it.

I share these anecdotes about my personal life experiences, as well as my flight into space, in auditoriums, in universities, and with businesses. My hope is that listeners will find inspiration within themselves as I found it when I learned of Franklin Chang Díaz's accomplishments. I always thought, "If he did it, why can't I?" and that is the same phrase I hope others will say when they read or hear of my story.

Moreover, I believe that doing my part to actively help others succeed is integral to building a generation of children who are growing up in one of our country's worst economic times. This, coupled with my lifelong passion for knowledge, is why I started—and am so committed to—the Reaching for the Stars Foundation. Since its inception in December 2005, the foundation has helped to engage students, as early as the fifth grade, in the science, technology, engineering, and mathematics (STEM) fields. Through a two-day Science Blast

Conference, Summer Academy, and scholarships, the foundation ensures that there are opportunities available through which children can pursue their educational and professional goals regardless of perceived obstacles.

Many people congratulate me on reaching my dreams. I have been told that I am "an astronaut who still has his feet on the ground." I think it is true. I continue to be the same José, the same Pepe, whom my parents, teachers, and friends have known for all of their lives. Yes, I am the guy who was able to reach his out-of-this-world goals, but I care about the same things as most people. I want to take care of and provide for my family, and I want to see my children grow up having access to opportunities that will allow them to be successful in life. I want to know that the American Dream is alive and well.

When I came back home to the Central Valley, I found my community to be a changed place. It was at the peak of the mortgage and foreclosure crisis, unemployment was roughly twice the national average, and the local congressman was ineffectively serving the very people whom he was elected to help. There was no question that faith needed to be restored in the American Dream. The only question was who should stand up and fight to make this possible.

I knew that I wanted to serve the people of my community one day, but it took being approached by President Obama to realize that the time to serve was now. At the Congressional Hispanic Caucus Institute's Awards Gala in September 2011, President Obama told me that I should seriously consider running for Congress because I would be a great candidate. The First Lady, Michelle Obama, said that she would happily come to the district and campaign for me. Coupled with the knowledge that I could bring my family back to our home, this presidential push helped me make the decision to accept the greater challenge that comes with serving one's community.

I have decided to go into this selflessly, realizing that my run for Congress is about securing the future of my community. I feel that I have a responsibility to ensure that all children, not just my own, can grow up and reach for the stars. I want to educate, motivate, and inspire young people—and really, all people—to dream about a life bigger than they could have ever imagined possible. It is my hope that my work in Congress, should I be elected, will help to make a better future for all people who call this great nation home.

My family and I have made the move from Houston, Texas, to Manteca, California. Adelita and I just celebrated our twentieth wedding anniversary. I fall more deeply in love with her each year that we spend together. We are so thankful for our family, and we are truly blessed to see each of our children discover their own dreams. Our philosophy has been that we should inspire, support, and encourage our children to harvest their own stars.

Our eldest, Julio Andres, is now seventeen and an Eagle Scout. He just graduated high school and earned an associate in arts degree in science. Julio is going off to college in the fall to study mechanical engineering. Karina Isabel is sixteen, and she wants to go into education. Vanessa Adelita is fifteen, and she likes math and acting. The brainiac of the bunch, Yesenia Marisol, is now thirteen. Antonio Miguel—who I am convinced is my doppelganger—is nine and wants to be a doctor. I now anxiously await the pathways that my five children, my five little stars, will take—all the while holding the hand of my beloved Adelita, who is my partner, my love, my confidante, and my strength.

So what will tomorrow bring? I honestly do not know. Congress, perhaps? But for now, I continue living, working, and waiting for all that is yet to come. I am intrigued by what the future holds, optimistic about the endless possibilities that lie ahead. Regardless, I do know one thing that is certain: Fueled by my passion to help everyone reach for the stars and my mission to make tomorrow better than today, I dedicate myself to a life of service.

Thank you for letting me share my journey with you. I wish you the best of luck in harvesting your own stars—in achieving your own dreams!

Follow me on Twitter at @Astro_Jose.

Learn more about the Reaching for the Stars Foundation by visiting www.astrojh.com.